NEWMAN ON LENT

JOHN HENRY CARDINAL NEWMAN

NEWMAN
on LENT

Meditations and Sermons

SOPHIA INSTITUTE PRESS

Manchester, New Hampshire

Sophia Institute Press
Box 5284, Manchester, NH 03108
1-800-888-9344
www.SophiaInstitute.com

Sophia Institute Press is a registered trademark of Sophia Institute.

paperback ISBN 979-8-88911-308-9

ebook ISBN 979-8-88911-309-6

Library of Congress Control Number: 2024949646

First printing

Contents

MEDITATIONS ON LENT: HOPE IN GOD, REDEEMER

CHAPTER 1

The Mental Sufferings of Our Lord

AUGUST 18, 1855

1. AFTER ALL HIS discourses were consummated, fully finished, and brought to an end, then He said, "The Son of man will be betrayed to crucifixion" (see Matt. 26:1–2). As an army puts itself in battle array, as sailors, before an action, clear the decks, as dying men make their will and then turn to God, so though our Lord could never cease to speak good words, did He sum up and complete His teaching and then commence His Passion. Then He removed by His own act the prohibition that kept Satan from Him and opened the door to the agitations of His human heart, as a soldier who is to suffer death may drop his handkerchief himself. At once Satan came on and seized upon his brief hour.

2. An evil temper of murmuring and criticism is spread among the disciples. One was the source of it, but it seems to have been spread. The thought of His death was before Him, and He was thinking of it and His burial after it. A woman came and anointed His sacred head. The action spread a soothing tender feeling over His pure soul. It was a mute token of sympathy, and the whole house was filled with it. It was rudely broken by the harsh voice of the traitor now for the first time giving utterance to his secret heartlessness and malice. *Ut quid perditio haec?* "To

what purpose is this waste?" — the unjust steward with his impious economy making up for his own private thefts by grudging honor to his Master. Thus, in the midst of the sweet, calm harmony of that feast at Bethany, there comes a jar and discord; all is wrong: sour discontent and distrust are spreading, for the devil is abroad.

3. Judas, having once shown what he was, lost no time in carrying out his malice. He went to the chief priests and bargained with them to betray his Lord for a price. Our Lord saw all that took place within him; He saw Satan knocking at his heart and admitted there and made an honored and beloved guest and an intimate. He saw him go to the priests and heard the conversation between them. He had seen it by His foreknowledge all the time he had been about Him, and when He chose him. What we know feebly as to be affects us far more vividly and very differently when it actually takes place. Our Lord had at length felt, and suffered Himself to feel, the cruelty of the ingratitude of which He was the sport and victim. He had treated Judas as one of His most familiar friends. He had shown marks of the closest intimacy; He had made him the purse-keeper of Himself and His followers. He had given him the power of working miracles. He had admitted him to a knowledge of the mysteries of the Kingdom of Heaven. He had sent him out to preach and had made him one of His own special representatives so that the Master was judged by the conduct of His servant. A heathen, when smitten by a friend, said, "*Et tu Brute!*" What desolation is in the sense of ingratitude! God, who is met with ingratitude daily, cannot from His Nature feel it. He took a human heart so that He might feel it in its fullness. And now, O my God, though in Heaven, dost Thou not feel my ingratitude toward Thee?

MARCH 10

4. I see the figure of a man, whether young or old I cannot tell. He may be fifty or he may be thirty. Sometimes He looks one, sometimes the other. There is something inexpressible about His face that I cannot solve. Perhaps, as He bears all burdens, He bears that of old age too. But so it is; His face is at once most venerable, yet most childlike, most calm, most sweet, most modest, beaming with sanctity and with loving kindness. His eyes rivet me and move my heart. His breath is all fragrant and transports me out of myself. Oh, I will look upon that face forever and will not cease.

5. And I see suddenly someone come to Him and raise his hand and sharply strike Him on that heavenly face. It is a hard hand, the hand of a rude man, and perhaps has iron upon it. It could not be so sudden as to take Him by surprise who knows all things past and future, and He shows no sign of resentment, remaining calm and grave as before; but the expression of His face is marred; a great wheal arises, and in a little time that all-gracious face is hid from me by the effects of this indignity, as if a cloud came over it.

6. A hand was lifted up against the face of Christ. Whose hand was that? My conscience tells me, "Thou art the man." I trust it is not so with me now. But, O my soul, contemplate the awful fact. Fancy Christ before thee, and fancy thyself lifting up thy hand and striking Him! Thou wilt say, "It is impossible: I could not do so." Yes, thou hast done so. When thou didst sin willfully, then thou hast done so. He is beyond pain now: still thou hast struck Him, and had it been in the days of His flesh, He would have felt pain. Turn back in memory, and recollect the time, the day, the hour, when by willful mortal sin, by scoffing at sacred things, or by profaneness, or by dark hatred of this thy Brother, or by acts of impurity, or by deliberate rejection of God's voice, or in any other devilish way known to thee, thou hast struck the All-holy One.

O injured Lord, what can I say? I am very guilty concerning Thee, my Brother; and I shall sink in sullen despair if Thou dost not raise me. I cannot look on Thee; I shrink from Thee; I throw my arms round my face; I crouch to the earth. Satan will pull me down if Thou take not pity. It is terrible to turn to Thee; but oh turn Thou me, and so shall I be turned. It is a purgatory to endure the sight of Thee, the sight of myself — I most vile, Thou most holy. Yet make me look once more on Thee whom I have so incomprehensibly affronted, for Thy countenance is my only life, my only hope and health lies in looking on Thee whom I have pierced. So I put myself before Thee; I look on Thee again; I endure the pain in order to the purification.

O my God, how can I look Thee in the face when I think of my ingratitude, so deeply seated, so habitual, so immovable — or rather so awfully increasing! Thou loadest me day by day with Thy favors and feedest me with Thyself, as Thou didst Judas, yet I not only do not profit thereby but I do not even make any acknowledgment at the time. Lord, how long? When shall I be free from this real, this fatal captivity? He who made Judas his prey has got foothold of me in my old age, and I cannot get loose. It is the same day after day. When wilt Thou give me a still greater grace than Thou hast given, the grace to profit by the graces that Thou givest? When wilt Thou give me Thy effectual grace that alone can give life and vigor to this effete, miserable, dying soul of mine? My God, I know not in what sense I can pain Thee in Thy glorified state; but I know that every fresh sin, every fresh ingratitude I now commit, was among the blows and stripes that once fell on Thee in Thy Passion. Oh let me have as little share in those Thy past sufferings as possible. Day by day goes, and I find I have been more and more, by the new sins of each day, the cause of them. I know that at best I have a real share *in solido* of them all, but still it is shocking to find myself having a greater and greater share. Let others wound Thee — let not me. Let not me have to think that Thou wouldest have had this or that pang of soul or body the less, except for me. O my God, I am so fast in prison that I cannot get out. O Mary, pray for me. O Philip, pray for me, though I do not deserve Thy pity.

CHAPTER 2

Our Lord Refuses Sympathy

1. SYMPATHY MAY BE called an eternal law, for it is signified or rather transcendentally and archetypically fulfilled in the ineffable mutual love of the divine Trinity. God, though infinitely One, has ever been Three. He ever has rejoiced in His Son and His Spirit, and they in Him — and thus through all eternity He has existed, not solitary, though alone, having in this incomprehensible multiplication of Himself and reiteration of His Person such infinitely perfect bliss that nothing He has created can add aught to it. The devil only is barren and lonely, shut up in himself — and his servants also.

2. When, for our sakes, the Son came on earth and took our flesh, yet He would not live without the sympathy of others. For thirty years, He lived with Mary and Joseph and thus formed a shadow of the Heavenly Trinity on earth. Oh the perfection of that sympathy that existed between the three! Not a look of one but the other two understood, as expressed, better than if expressed in a thousand words — nay, more than understood: accepted, echoed, corroborated. It was like three instruments absolutely in tune that all vibrate when one vibrates and vibrate either one and the same note or in perfect harmony.

3. The first weakening of that unison was when Joseph died. It was no jar in the sound, for to the last moment of his life, he was

one with them, and the sympathy between the three only became more intense and more sweet while it was brought into new circumstances, and it had a wider range in the months of his declining, his sickness, and death. Then it was like an air ranging through a number of notes performed perfectly and exactly in time and tune by all three. But it ended in a lower note than before, and when Joseph went, a weaker one. Not that Joseph, though so saintly, added much in volume of sound to the other two, but sympathy, by its very meaning, implies number, and, on his death, one, out of three harps, was unstrung and silent.

4. Oh what a moment of sympathy between the three, the moment before Joseph died — they supporting and hanging over him, he looking at them and reposing in them with undivided, unreserved, supreme devotion, for he was in the arms of God and the Mother of God. As a flame shoots up and expires, so was the ecstasy of that last moment ineffable, for each knew and thought of the reverse that was to follow on the snapping of that bond. One moment, very different, of joy, not of sorrow, was equal to it in intensity of feeling, that of the birth of Jesus. The birth of Jesus, the death of Joseph, moments of unutterable sweetness, unparalleled in the history of mankind. St. Joseph went to limbo, to wait his time out of God's Presence. Jesus had to preach, suffer, and die; Mary to witness His sufferings and, even after He had risen again, to go on living without Him amid the changes of life and the heartlessness of the heathen.

5. The birth of Jesus, the death of Joseph: those moments of transcendentally pure and perfect and living sympathy between the three members of this earthly Trinity were its beginning and its end. The death of Joseph, which broke it up, was the breaking up of more than itself. It was but the beginning of that change that was coming over Son and Mother. Going on now for thirty years, each

of them had been preserved from the world and had lived for each other. Now He had to go out to preach and suffer, and — as the foremost and most inevitable of His trials, and one that from first to last He voluntarily undertook, even when not imperative — He deprived Himself of the enjoyment of that intercommunion of hearts — of His heart with the heart of Mary — that had been His from the time He took man's nature, and that He had possessed in an archetypal and transcendent manner with His Father and His Spirit from all eternity.

O my soul, thou art allowed to contemplate this union of the three and to share thyself its sympathy, by faith though not by sight. My God, I believe and know that then a communion of heavenly things was opened on earth that has never been suspended. It is my duty and my bliss to enter into it myself. It is my duty and my bliss to be in tune with that most touching music that then began to sound. Give me that grace that alone can make me hear and understand it, that it may thrill through me. Let the breathings of my soul be with Jesus, Mary, and Joseph. Let me live in obscurity, out of the world and the world's thought, with them. Let me look to them in sorrow and in joy, and live and die in their sweet sympathy.

6. The *last* day of the earthly intercourse between Jesus and Mary was at the marriage feast at Cana. Yet even then there was something taken from that blissful intimacy, for they no longer lived simply for each other but showed themselves in public and began to take their place in the dispensation that was opening. He manifested forth His glory by His first miracle — and hers also by making her intercession the medium of it. He honored her still more by breaking through the appointed order of things for her sake and, though His time of miracles was not come, anticipating it at her instance. While He wrought His miracle, however, He took leave of her in the words "Woman, what is between thee and Me?" (John 2:4). Thus He

parted with her absolutely, though He parted with a blessing. It was leaving Paradise feeble and alone.

7. For in truth it was fitting that He who was to be the true High Priest should thus, while He exercised His office for the whole race of man, be free from all human ties and sympathies of the flesh. And one reason for His long abode at Nazareth with His Mother may have been to show that as He gave up His Father's and His own glory on high to become man, so He gave up the innocent and pure joys of His earthly home in order that He might be a Priest. So, in the old time, Melchizedek is described as without father or mother. So the Levites showed themselves truly worthy of the sacerdotal office and were made the sacerdotal tribe because they steeled themselves against natural affection, said to father or mother, "I know you not," and raised the sword against their own kindred when the honor of the Lord of armies demanded the sacrifice. In like manner our Lord said to Mary, "What is between Me and thee?" It was the setting apart of the sacrifice, the first ritual step of the Great Act that was to be solemnly performed for the salvation of the world. "What is between Me and thee, O woman?" is the offertory before the oblation of the Host. O my dear Lord, Thou who hast given up Thy mother for me, give me grace cheerfully to give up all my earthly friends and relations for Thee.

8. The Great High Priest said to His kindred, "I know you not." Then, as He did so, we may believe that the most tender heart of Jesus looked back upon His whole time since His birth and called before Him those former days of His infancy and childhood, when He had been with others from whom He had long been parted. Time was when St. Elizabeth and the Holy Baptist had formed part of the Holy Family. St. Elizabeth, like St. Joseph, had been removed by death and was waiting His coming to break that bond that detained both her and St. Joseph from Heaven. St. John had been cut off from

his home and mankind — and the sympathies of earth, long since — and had now begun to preach the coming Savior and was waiting and expecting His manifestation.

Give me grace, O Jesus, to live in sight of that blessed company. Let my life be spent in the presence of Thee and Thy dearest friends. Though I see them not, let not what I do see seduce me to give my heart elsewhere. Because Thou hast blessed me so much and given to me friends, let me not depend or rely or throw myself in any way upon them, but in Thee be my life, and my conversation and daily walk among those with whom Thou didst surround Thyself on earth and dost now delight Thyself in Heaven. Be my soul with Thee and, because with Thee, with Mary and Joseph and Elizabeth and John.

9. Nor did He, as time went on, give up Mary and Joseph only. There still remained to Him invisible attendants and friends, and He had their sympathy, but them He at length gave up also. From the time of His birth we may suppose He held communion with the spirits of the Old Fathers who had prepared His coming and prophesied of it. On one occasion He was seen all through the night conversing with Moses and Elijah, and that conversation was about His Passion. What a field of thought is thus opened to us, of which we know how little. When He passed whole nights in prayer, it was greater refreshment to soul and body than sleep. Who could support and (so to say) reinvigorate the divine Lord better than that "*laudabilis numerus*" of prophets of which He was the fulfillment and antitype? Then He might talk with Abraham, who saw His day, or Moses, who spoke to Him; or with His especial types, David and Jeremiah; or with those who spoke most of Him, as Isaiah and Daniel. And here was a fund of great sympathy. When He came up to Jerusalem to suffer, He might be met in spirit by all the holy priests who had offered sacrifices in shadow of Him; just as now the priest recalls in Mass the sacrifices of Abel, Abraham, and Melchizedek and

the fiery gift that purged the lips of Isaiah, as well as holding communion with the apostles and martyrs.

10. Let us linger for a while with Mary before we follow the steps of her Son, our Lord. There was an occasion when He refused leave to one who would bid his own home farewell, before he followed Him; and such was, as it seems, almost His own way with His Mother; but will He be displeased if we one instant stop with her, though our meditation lies with Him? O Mary, we are devout to thy seven woes — but was not this, though not one of those seven, one of the greatest and included those that followed from thy knowledge of them beforehand? How didst thou bear that first separation from Him? How did the first days pass when thou wast desolate? Where didst thou hide thyself? Where didst thou pass the long three years and more while He was on His ministry? Once — at the beginning of it — thou didst attempt to get near Him, and then we hear nothing of thee till we find thee standing at His Cross. And then, after that great joy of seeing Him again, and the permanent consolation, never to be lost, that with Him all suffering and humiliation was over and that never had she to weep for Him again, still she was separated from Him for many years while she lived in the flesh, surrounded by the wicked world, and in the misery of His absence.

11. The blessed Mary, among her other sorrows, suffered the loss of her Son after He had lived under the same roof with her for thirty years. When He was no more than twelve, He gave her a token of what was to be and said, "I must be about my Father's business" (Luke 2:49); and when the time came and He began His miracles, He said to her, "What is to Me and to thee?" — What is common to us two? — and soon He left her. Once she tried to see Him, but in vain, and she could not reach Him for the crowd, and He made no effort to receive her nor said a kind word; and then, at the last, once more she tried, and she reached Him in time to see Him hanging on

the Cross and dying. He was only forty days on earth after His Resurrection, and then He left her in old age to finish her life without Him. Compare her thirty happy years and her time of desolation.

12. I see her in her forlorn home while her Son and Lord was going up and down the land without a place to lay His head, suffering both because she was so desolate and He was so exposed. How dreary passed the day; and then came reports that He was in some peril or distress. She heard, perhaps, He had been led into the wilderness to be tempted. She would have shared all His sufferings but was not permitted. Once there was a profane report that was believed by many that He was beside Himself, and His friends and kindred went out to get possession of Him. She went out, too, to see Him and tried to reach Him. She could not for the crowd. A message came to Him to that effect, but He made no effort to receive her, nor said a kind word. She went back to her home disappointed, without the sight of Him. And so she remained, perhaps in company with those who did not believe in Him.

13. I see her, too, after His Ascension. This, too, is a time of bereavement, but still of consolation. It was still a twilight time, but not a time of grief. The Lord was absent, but He was not on earth, He was not in suffering. Death had no power over Him. And He came to her day by day in the Blessed Sacrifice. I see the Blessed Mary at Mass and St. John celebrating. She is waiting for the moment of her Son's Presence: now she converses with Him in the sacred rite; and what shall I say now? She receives Him to whom once she gave birth.

O Holy Mother, stand by me now at Mass time when Christ comes to me, as thou didst minister to Thy Infant Lord — as thou didst hang upon His words when He grew up, as thou wast found under His Cross. Stand by me, Holy Mother, that I may gain somewhat of thy purity, thy innocence, thy faith, and He may be the one object of my love and my adoration, as He was of thine.

14. There were others who more directly ministered to Him, and of whom we are told more — the holy angels. It was the voice of the archangel that announced to the prophet His coming that consigned the Eternal to the womb of Mary. Angels hymned His nativity, and all the angels of God worshipped at His crib. An angel sent Him into Egypt and brought Him back. Angels ministered to Him after His temptation. Angels wrought His miracles when He did not will to exert His Almighty *fiat*. But He bade them go at length, as He had bidden His Mother go. One remained at His agony. Afterward, He said, "Think ye not I could pray to My Father, and He would send me myriads of angels?" — implying that in fact His guards had been withdrawn (Matt. 26:53). The Church prays Him, on His Ascension, "King of Glory, Lord of Angels, leave us not orphans." He, the Lord of Angels, was at this time despoiled of them.

15. He took other human friends when He had given up His Mother — the twelve apostles — as if He desired that in which He might sympathize. He chose them, as He says, to be "not servants but friends" (John 15:15). He made them His confidants. He told them things that He did not tell others. It was His will to favor, nay, to indulge them, as a father behaves toward a favorite child. He made them more blessed than kings and prophets and wise men from the things He told them. He called them His "little ones" and preferred them for His gifts to the wise and prudent. He exulted, while He praised them, that they had continued with Him in His temptations, and as if in gratitude He announced that they should sit upon twelve thrones judging the twelve tribes of Israel. He rejoiced in their sympathy when His solemn trial was approaching. He assembled them about Him at the Last Supper as if they were to support Him in it. "With desire," He says, "have I desired to eat this Pasch with you, before I suffer" (Luke 22:15). Thus there was an interchange of good offices and an intimate sympathy between

them. But it was His adorable will that they too should leave Him, that He should be left to Himself. One betrayed, another denied Him, the rest ran away from Him and left Him in the hands of His enemies. Even after He had risen, none would believe in it. Thus He trod the winepress alone.

16. He who was Almighty and All-blessed, and who flooded His own soul with the full glory of the vision of His divine nature, would still subject that soul to all the infirmities that naturally belonged to it; and as He suffered it to rejoice in the sympathy and to be desolate under the absence of human friends, so, when it pleased Him, He could, and did, deprive it of the light of the presence of God. This was the last and crowning misery that He put upon it. He had in the course of His ministry fled from man to God; he had appealed to Him; He had taken refuge from the rude ingratitude of the race whom He was saving in divine communion. He retired of nights to pray. He said, "the Father loveth the Son, and shews to Him all things that He doth Himself" (John 5:20). He returned thanks to Him for hiding His mysteries from the wise to reveal them to the little ones. But now He deprived Himself of this elementary consolation by which He lived, and that not in part only but in its fullness. He said when His Passion began, "My soul is sorrowful even unto death" (Matt. 26:38); and at the last, "My God, why hast Thou forsaken Me?" (Matt. 27:46). Thus He was stripped of all things.

My God and Savior, who wast thus deprived of the light of consolation, whose soul was dark, whose affections were left to thirst without the true object of them, and all this for man, take not from *me* the light of Thy countenance, lest I shrivel from the loss of it and perish in my infirmity. Who can sustain the loss of the Sun of the soul but Thou? Who can walk without light, or labor without the pure air, but Thy great saints? As for me, alas, I shall turn to the creature for my comfort, if Thou wilt not give me Thyself. I shall not mourn, I shall not hunger or thirst after justice, but I shall look about for whatever is at hand, and feed on offal, or stay my appetite with husks, ashes, or chaff, which if they poison me not, at least nourish not. O my God, leave me not in that dry state in which I am; give me the comfort of Thy grace. How can I have any tenderness or sweetness unless I have Thee to look upon? How can I continue in prayer, as is my duty doubly, since I belong to the Oratory, unless Thou encourage me and make it pleasant to me? It is hardly that an old man keeps any warmth in him; it is slowly that he recovers what is lost. Yet, O my God, St. Philip is my father — and he seems never in his life to have been desolate. Thou didst give him trials, but didst Thou ever take from him the light of Thy countenance! O Philip, wilt thou not gain for me some tithe of thy own peace and joy, thy cheerfulness, thy gentleness, and thy self-denying charity? I am in all things the most opposite to thee, yet I represent thee.

Chapter 3

The Bodily Sufferings of Our Lord

April 19, Wednesday in Holy Week

1. His bodily pains were greater than those of any martyr because He willed them to be greater. All pain of body depends, as to be felt at all so to be felt in this or that degree, on the nature of the living mind that dwells in that body. Vegetables have no feeling because they have no living mind or spirit within them. Brute animals feel more or less according to the intelligence within them. Man feels more than any brute because he has a soul; Christ's soul felt more than that of any other man because His soul was exalted by personal union with the Word of God.[1] Christ felt bodily pain more keenly than any other man, as much as man feels pain more keenly than any other animal.

2. It is a relief to pain to have the thoughts drawn another way. Thus, soldiers in battle often do not know when they are wounded. Again, persons in raging fevers seem to suffer a great deal; then afterward they can but recollect general discomfort and restlessness. And

---

[1] Here Newman is referring to Christ's human soul being united to His divine nature in the person of the Second Person of the Trinity. See also Newman's "Discourse 16. Mental Sufferings of Our Lord in His Passion": "You know, my brethren, that our Lord and Savior, though He was God, was also perfect man; and hence He had not only a body, but a soul likewise, such as ours, though pure from all stain of evil." — Editor's note.

so excitement and enthusiasm are great alleviations of bodily pain; thus savages die at the stake singing songs amid torments; it is a sort of mental drunkenness. And so again an instantaneous pain is comparatively bearable; it is the continuance of pain that is so heavy, and if we had no memory of the pain we suffered last minute, and also suffer in the present, we should find pain easy to bear; but what makes the second pang grievous is because there has been a first pang; and what makes the third more grievous is that there has been a first and second; the pain seems to grow because it is prolonged. Now Christ suffered not as in a delirium or in excitement or in inadvertency, but He looked pain in the face! He offered His whole mind to it and received it, as it were, directly into His bosom, and He suffered all He suffered with a full consciousness of suffering.

3. Christ would not drink the drugged cup that was offered to Him to cloud His mind. He willed to have the full sense of pain. His soul was so intently fixed on His suffering as not to be distracted from it; and it was so active, and it recollected the past and anticipated the future, and the whole Passion was, as it were, concentrated on each moment of it, and all that He had suffered and all that He was to suffer lent its aid to increase what He was suffering. Yet withal His soul was so calm and sober and unexcited as to be passive and thus to receive the full burden of the pain on it without the power of throwing it off Him. Moreover, the sense of conscious innocence, and the knowledge that His sufferings would come to an end, might have supported Him; but He repressed the comfort and turned away His thoughts from these alleviations that He might suffer absolutely and perfectly.

O my God and Savior, who went through such sufferings for me with such lively consciousness, such precision, such recollection, and such fortitude, enable me, by Thy help, if I am brought into the power of this terrible trial, bodily pain, enable me to bear it with some portion of Thy calmness. Obtain for me this grace, O Virgin Mother, who didst see thy Son suffer and didst suffer with Him; that I, when I suffer, may associate my sufferings with His and with thine, and that through His Passion, and thy merits and those of all saints, they may be a satisfaction for my sins and procure for me eternal life.

Maundy Thursday

4. Our Lord's sufferings were so great because His soul was in suffering. What shows this is that His soul began to suffer before His bodily Passion, as we see in the agony in the garden. The first anguish that came upon His body was not from without — it was not from the scourges, the thorns, or the nails, but from His soul. His soul was in such agony that He called it death: "My soul is sorrowful even unto death" (Matt. 26:38). The anguish was such that it, as it were, burst open His whole body. It was a pang affecting His heart, as in the deluge the floods of the great deep were broken up and the windows of Heaven were open. The blood, rushing from His tormented heart, forced its way on every side, formed for itself a thousand new channels, filled all the pores, and at length stood forth upon His skin in thick drops that fell heavily on the ground.

5. He remained in this living death from the time of His agony in the garden; and as His first agony was from His soul, so was His last. As the scourge and the Cross did not begin His sufferings, so they did not close them. It was the agony of His soul, not of His body, that caused His death. His persecutors were surprised to hear that He was dead. How, then, did He die? That agonized, tormented heart, which at the beginning so awfully relieved itself in the rush of blood and the bursting of His pores, at length broke. It broke, and He died. It would have broken *at once* had He not kept it from breaking. At length the moment came. He gave the word, and His heart broke.

6. O tormented heart, it was love and sorrow and fear that broke Thee. It was the sight of human sin, it was the sense of it, the feeling of it laid on Thee; it was zeal for the glory of God, horror at seeing sin so near Thee, a sickening, stifling feeling at its pollution, the deep shame and disgust and abhorrence and revolt that it inspired, keen pity for the souls whom it has drawn headlong into Hell — all these feelings together Thou didst allow to rush upon Thee. Thou didst submit Thyself to their powers, and they were Thy death. That strong heart, that all-noble, all-generous, all-tender, all-pure heart was slain by sin.

O most tender and gentle Lord Jesus, when will my heart have a portion of Thy perfections? When will my hard and stony heart, my proud heart, my unbelieving, my impure heart, my narrow and self-ish heart, be melted and conformed to Thine? O teach me so to contemplate Thee that I may become like Thee, and to love Thee sincerely and simply as Thou hast loved me.

CHAPTER 4

It Is Consummated

APRIL 22

1. IT IS OVER now, O Lord, as with Thy sufferings, so with our humiliations. We have followed Thee from Thy fasting in the wilderness till Thy death on the Cross. For forty days we have professed to do penance. The time has been long and it has been short; but whether long or short, it is now over. It is over, and we feel a pleasure that it is over; it is a relief and a release. We thank Thee that it is over. We thank Thee for the time of sorrow, but we thank Thee more as we look forward to the time of festival. Pardon our shortcomings in Lent and reward us in Easter.

2. We have, indeed, done very little for Thee, O Lord. We recollect well our listlessness and weariness; our indisposition to mortify ourselves when we had no plea of health to stand in the way; our indisposition to pray and to meditate — our disorder of mind — our discontent, our peevishness. Yet some of us, perhaps, have done something for Thee. Look on us as a whole, O Lord, look on us as a community, and let what some have done well plead for us all.

3. O Lord, the end is come. We are conscious of our languor and lukewarmness; we do not deserve to rejoice in Easter, yet we cannot help doing so. We feel more of pleasure, we rejoice in Thee more than our past humiliation warrants us in doing; yet may that

very joy be its own warrant. Oh be indulgent to us, for the merits of Thy own all-powerful Passion, and for the merits of Thy saints. Accept us as Thy little flock, in the day of small things, in a fallen country, in an age when faith and love are scarce. Pity us and spare us and give us peace.

O my own Savior, now in the tomb but soon to arise, Thou hast paid the price; it is done — *consummatum est* — it is secured. Oh fulfill Thy Resurrection in us, and as Thou hast purchased us, claim us, take possession of us, make us Thine.

SERMONS ON LENT

Chapter 1

Bodily Suffering

"I fill up that which is behind of the afflictions of Christ
in my flesh for His body's sake, which is the Church."

Colossians 1:24

Our Lord and Savior Jesus Christ came by blood as well as by water, not only as a Fount of grace and truth — the source of spiritual light, joy, and salvation — but as a combatant with Sin and Satan who was consecrated through suffering. He was, as prophecy had marked Him out, "red in His apparel, and His garments like Him that treadeth in the winefat" (Isa. 63:2); or, in the words of the apostle, "He was clothed with a vesture dipped in blood" (Rev. 19:13). It was the untold sufferings of the Eternal Word in our nature, His body dislocated and torn, His blood poured out, His soul violently separated by a painful death, that has put away from us the wrath of Him whose love sent Him for that very purpose. This only was our Atonement; no one shared in the work. He "trod the winepress alone, and of the people there was none with Him" (Isa. 63:3). When lifted up upon the cursed tree, He fought with all the hosts of evil and conquered by suffering. Thus, in a most mysterious way, all that is needful for this sinful world, the life of our souls, the regeneration of our nature, all that is most joyful and glorious, hope, light, peace, spiritual freedom, holy influences, religious knowledge and strength, all flow from a fount of blood. A work of blood is our salvation; and we, as we would be saved, must draw near and gaze upon it in faith and accept it as the way to Heaven. We must take Him, who thus suffered, as our guide; we must embrace His sacred feet and follow Him. No wonder, then, should we receive on ourselves some drops of the sacred agony that bedewed His garments; no wonder should we be sprinkled with the sorrows that He bore in expiation of our sins!

And so it has ever been in very deed; to approach Him has been, from the first, to be partaker, more or less, in His sufferings; I do not say in the case of every individual who believes in Him, but as regards the more conspicuous, the more favored, His choice instruments, and His most active servants; that is, it has been the lot of the Church, on the whole, and of those, on the whole, who had been most like Him, as Rulers, Intercessors, and Teachers of the Church. He, indeed, alone meritoriously; they, because they have been near Him. Thus, immediately upon His birth, He brought the sword upon the infants of His own age at Bethlehem. His very shadow, cast upon a city where He did not abide, was stained with blood. His Blessed Mother had not clasped Him to her breast for many weeks ere she was warned of the penalty of that fearful privilege: "Yea, a sword shall pierce through thy own soul also" (Luke 2:35). Virtue went out of Him; but the water and the blood flowed together as afterward from His pierced side. From among the infants He took up in His arms to bless is said to have gone forth a chief martyr of the generation after Him. Most of His apostles passed through lifelong sufferings to a violent death. In particular, when the favored brothers, James and John, came to Him with a request that they might sit beside Him in His Kingdom, He plainly stated this connection between nearness to Him and affliction:

"Are ye able," He said, "to drink of the cup that I shall drink of, and to be baptized with the baptism that I am baptized with?" (Matt. 20:22). As if He said, "Ye cannot have the sacraments of grace without the painful figures of them. The Cross, when imprinted on your foreheads, will draw blood. You shall receive, indeed, the Baptism of the Spirit, and the cup of My Communion, but it shall be with the attendant pledges of My cup of agony and My baptism of blood." Elsewhere He speaks the same language to all who would partake the benefits of His death and Passion: "Whosoever doth not bear his cross, and come after Me, cannot be My disciple" (Luke 14:27).

Accordingly, His apostles frequently remind us of this necessary, though mysterious, appointment and bid us "think it not strange concerning the fiery trial which is to try you, as though some strange thing happened unto you," but to rejoice in having communion with the sufferings of Christ (1 Pet. 4:12–13). Paul teaches us the same lesson in the text, in which he speaks of taking up the remnant of Christ's sorrows, as some precious mantle dropped from the Cross, and wearing it for His sake: "I rejoice in my sufferings for you, and fill up in my flesh what remains of the afflictions of Christ for His body's sake, that is, the Church" (Col. 1:24; see also 2 Cor. 4:10). And though he is speaking especially of persecution and other sufferings borne in the cause of the Gospel, yet it is our great privilege, as Scripture tells us, that all pain and trouble, borne in faith and patience, will be accounted as marks of Christ, grace-tokens from the absent Savior, and will be accepted and rewarded for His sake at the Last Day. It declares generally, "When thou passest through the waters, I will be with thee; and through the rivers, they shall not overflow thee: when thou walkest through the fire, thou shalt not be burned; neither shall the flame kindle upon thee" (Isa. 43:2); and "Our light affliction, which is but for a moment, worketh for us a far more exceeding and eternal weight of glory" (2 Cor. 4:17).

Thus the Gospel, which has shed light in so many ways upon the state of this world, has aided especially our view of the sufferings to which human nature is subjected, turning a punishment into a privilege in the case of all pain, and especially of bodily pain, which is the most mysterious of all. Sorrow, anxiety, and disappointment are more or less connected with sin and sinners; but bodily pain is involuntary for the most part, stretching over the world by some external, irresistible law, reaching to children who have never actually sinned and to the brute animals who are strangers to Adam's nature, while in its manifestations it is far more piteous and distressing than any other suffering. It is the lot of all of us, sooner or later, and that perhaps in a measure that it would be appalling and wrong to anticipate, whether from disease or from the casualties of life. And all of us at length must die; and death is generally ushered in by disease and ends in that separation of soul and body that itself may, in some cases, involve peculiar pain.

Worldly men put such thoughts aside as gloomy; they can neither deny nor avert the prospect before them; and they are wise, on their own principles, not to embitter the present by anticipating it. But Christians may bear to look at it without undue apprehension; for this very infliction, which most touches the heart and imagination, has (as I have said) been invested by Almighty God with a new and comfortable light as being the medium of His choicest mercies toward us. Pain is no longer a curse, a necessary evil to be undergone with a dry submission or passive endurance — it may be considered even as a blessing of the Gospel; and being a blessing, it admits of being met well or ill. In the way of nature, indeed, it seems to shut out the notion of duty, as if so masterful a discipline from without superseded the necessity or opportunity of self-mastery; but now that "Christ hath suffered in the flesh," we are bound "to arm ourselves with the same mind" (1 Pet. 4:1), and to obey, as He did, amid suffering.

In what follows, I shall remark briefly on the natural effect of pain upon the mind and upon the remedies and correctives of that effect that the knowledge of the Gospel supplies.

First, as to its effect upon the mind, let it be well understood that pain has no sanctifying influence in itself. Bad men are made worse by it. This should be borne in mind lest we deceive ourselves; for sometimes we speak (at least the poor often so speak) as though present hardship and suffering were in some sense a ground of confidence in themselves as to our future prospects, whether as expiating our sins or bringing our hearts nearer to God. Nay, even the more religious among us may be misled to think that pain makes them better than it really does; for the effect of it at length, on any but very proud or ungovernable tempers, is to cause a languor and composure of mind that looks like resignation while it necessarily throws our reason upon the especial thought of God, our only stay in such times of trial. Doubtless it does really benefit the Christian, and in no scanty measure; and he may thank God who thus blesses it; only let him be cautious of measuring his spiritual state by the particular exercise of faith and love in his heart at the time, especially if that exercise be limited to the affections themselves and have no opportunity of showing itself in works. St. Paul speaks of chastisement "yielding afterward the peaceable fruit of righteousness" (Heb. 12:11), formed indeed and ripened at the moment but manifested in due season. This may be the real fruit of the suffering of a deathbed, even though it may not have time to show itself to others before the Christian departs hence. Surely we may humbly hope that it perfects habits hitherto but partially formed and blends the several graces of the Spirit more entirely.

Such is the issue of it in established Christians — but it may possibly effect nothing so blessed. Nay, in the case of those who have followed Christ with but a half heart, it may be a trial too strong for their feebleness and may overpower them. This is a dreadful reflection for those who put off the day of repentance. Well does our Church pray for us: "Suffer us not, at our last hour, for any pains of death to fall from Thee!" As for unbelievers, we know how it affects them from such serious passages of Scripture as the following: "They gnawed their tongues for pain, and blasphemed the God of Heaven because of their pains and their sores, and repented not of their deeds" (Rev. 16:10–11).

Nay, I would go so far as to say not only that pain does not commonly improve us but that without care it has a strong tendency to do our souls harm, that is to say, by making us selfish: an effect produced even when it does us good in other ways. Weak health, for instance, instead of opening the heart, often makes a man supremely careful of his bodily ease and well-being. Men find an excuse in their infirmities for some extraordinary attention to their comforts; they consider they may fairly consult, on all occasions, their own convenience rather than that of another. They indulge their wayward wishes, allow themselves in indolence when they really might exert themselves, and think they may be fretful because they are weak. They become querulous, self-willed, fastidious, and egotistical. Bystanders, indeed, should be very cautious of thinking any particular sufferer to be thus minded, because, after all, sick people have a multitude of feelings that they cannot explain to anyone else and are often in the right in those matters in which they appear to others most fanciful or unreasonable. Yet this does not interfere with the correctness of my remark on the whole.

Take another instance under very different circumstances. If bodily suffering can be presented under distinct aspects, it is in the lassitude of a sickbed and in the hardships of the soldier's life. Yet of the latter we find selfishness almost a proverbial characteristic. Surely the life of soldiers on service is a very school of generosity and self-neglect, if rightly understood, and is used as such by the noble and high-principled; yet here, a low and carnal mind, instead of profiting by its advantages, will yield to the temptation of referring everything that befalls it to its own comfort and profit. To secure its own interests will become enshrined within it as its main duty, and with the greater plausibility, inasmuch as there is a sense in which it may really be so accounted. Others (it will suggest) must take care of themselves; it is a folly and weakness to think of them; there are but few chances of safety; the many must suffer, some unto death; it is wisdom to struggle for life and comfort and to dismiss the thought of others. Alas! Instances occur, every now and then, in the experience of life that show that such thoughts and feelings are not peculiar to any one class of men but are the actuating principles of the multitude. If an alarm of danger be given amid a crowd, the general eagerness for safety leads men to act toward each other with utter unconcern, if not with frantic cruelty. There are stories told of companies of men finding themselves at sea with scanty provisions and of the shocking deeds that followed when each was struggling to preserve his own life.

The natural effect, then, of pain and fear is to individualize us in our own minds, to fix our thoughts on ourselves, to make us selfish. It is through pain, chiefly, that we realize to ourselves even our bodily organs; a frame entirely without painful sensations is (as it were) one whole without parts and prefigures that future spiritual body that shall be the portion of the saints. And to this we most approximate in our youth, when we are not sensible that we are compacted of gross terrestrial matter, as advancing years convince us. The young reflect little upon themselves; they gaze around them, and live out of doors, and say they have souls, little under-standing their words. "They rejoice in their youth" (see Eccles. 11:9). This, then, is the effect of suffering, that it arrests us: that it puts, as it were, a finger upon us to ascertain for us our own individuality. But it does no more than this; if such a warning does not lead us through the stirrings of our conscience heavenward, it does but imprison us in ourselves and make us selfish.

Here, then, it is that the Gospel finds us: heirs to a visitation that, sooner or later, comes upon us, turning our thoughts from outward objects and so tempting us to idolize self, to the dishonor of that God whom we ought to worship and the neglect of man whom we should love as ourselves. Thus it finds us, and it obviates this danger not by removing pain but by giving it new associations. Pain, which by nature leads us only to ourselves, carries on the Christian mind from the thought of self to the contemplation of Christ, His Passion, His merits, and His pattern, and, thence, further to that united company of sufferers who follow Him and "are what He is in this world" (1 John 4:17). He is the great Object of our faith; and while we gaze upon Him, we learn to forget ourselves.

Surely that is not the most fearful and hateful of evils here below, however trying to the flesh, that Christ underwent voluntarily. No one chooses evil for its own sake but for the greater good wrought out through it. He underwent it as for ends greater than the immediate removal of it, "not grudgingly or of necessity," but cheerfully doing God's will, as the Gospel history sets before us (2 Cor. 9:7). When His time was come, we are told, "He steadfastly set His face to go to Jerusalem" (Luke 9:51). His disciples said, "Master, the Jews of late sought to stone Thee, and goest Thou thither again?" (John 11:8), but He persisted. Again, He said to Judas, "That thou doest, do quickly" (John 13:27). He proceeded to the garden beyond Cedron, though Judas knew the place (John 18:2); and when the band of officers came to seize Him, "He went forth, and said unto them … I am He" (John 18:4–5). And with what calmness and majesty did He bear His sufferings when they came upon Him, though by His agony in the garden He showed He fully felt their keenness! The psalmist, in his prediction of them, says, "I am poured out like water, and all my bones are out of joint; my heart is like wax, it is melted" (Ps. 22:14), describing, as it would seem, that sinking of spirit and enfeebling of nerve that severe pain causes. Yet in the midst of distress, which seemed to preclude the opportunity of obedience, He was "about His Father's business," even more diligently than when in His childhood He asked questions of the doctors in the Temple (Luke 2:49), not thinking to be merely passive under the trial but accounting it as if a great occasion for a noble and severe surrender of Himself to His Father's will. Thus He "learned obedience by the things which He suffered" (Heb. 5:8). Consider the deep and serene compassion that led Him to pray for those who crucified Him; His solicitous care of His Mother; and His pardoning words addressed to the robber who suffered with Him. And so, when He said, "It is finished" (John 19:30), He showed that He was still contemplating, with a clear intellect, "the travail of His soul, and was satisfied" (Isa. 53:11); and in the solemn surrender of Himself into His Father's hand, He showed where His mind rested in the midst of its darkness. Even when He seemed to be thinking of Himself and said, "I thirst" (John 19:28), He really was regarding the words of prophecy and was bent on vindicating, to the very letter, the divine announcements concerning Him. Thus, upon the Cross itself, we discern in Him the mercy of a Messenger from Heaven, the love and grace of a Savior, the dutifulness of a Son, the faith of a created nature, and the zeal of a servant of God. His mind was stayed upon His Father's sovereign will and infinite perfections, yet it could pass, without effort, to the claim of filial duty or the need of an individual sinner. Six out of His seven last words were words of faith and love. For one instant, a horrible dread overwhelmed Him, when He seemed to ask why God had forsaken Him (Matt. 27:46). Doubtless "that voice was for our sakes" (John 12:30), as when He made mention of His thirst; and, like the other, it was taken from inspired prophecy. Perhaps it was intended to set before us an example of a special trial to which human nature is subject, whatever was the real and inscrutable manner of it in Him who was all along supported by an inherent divinity; I mean the trial of sharp agony, hurrying the mind on to vague terrors and strange inexplicable thoughts and is, therefore, graciously recorded for our benefit in the history of His death, "who was tempted, in all points, like as we are, yet without sin" (Heb. 4:15).

Such, then, were our Lord's sufferings voluntarily undergone and ennobled by an active obedience, themselves the center of our hopes and worship yet borne without thought of self, toward God and for man. And who among us habitually dwells upon them but is led, without deliberate purpose, by the very warmth of gratitude and adoring love to attempt bearing his own inferior trials in the same heavenly mind? Who does not see that to bear pain well is to meet it courageously, not to shrink or waver but to pray for God's help, then to look at it steadfastly, to summon what nerve we have of mind and body, to receive its attack, and to bear up against it (while strength is given us) as against some visible enemy in close combat? Who will not acknowledge that, when sent to us, we must make its presence (as it were) our own voluntary act by the cheerful and ready concurrence of our own will with the will of God? Nay, who is there but must own that with Christ's sufferings before us, pain and tribulation are, after all, not only the most blessed but even the most congruous attendants upon those who are called to inherit the benefit of them? Most congruous, I say, not as though necessary but as most natural and befitting, harmonizing most fully, with the main Object in the group of sacred wonders on which the Church is called to gaze. Who, on the other hand, does not at least perceive that all the glare and gaudiness of this world, its excitements, its keenly pursued goods, its successes and its transports, its pomps and its luxuries, are not in character with that pale and solemn scene that faith must ever have in its eye? What Christian will not own that to "reign as kings" and to be "full" is not his calling (Rom. 5:17; Eph. 3:19), so as to derive comfort in the hour of sickness, or bereavement, or other affliction from the thought that he is now in his own place, if he be Christ's, in his true home, the sepulcher in which his Lord was laid? So deeply have His saints felt this that when times were peaceful and the Church was in safety, they could not rest in the lap of ease and have secured to themselves hardnesses lest the world should corrupt them. They could not bear to see the much-enduring Paul adding to his necessary tribulations a self-inflicted chastisement of the flesh and yet allow themselves to live delicately and fare sumptuously every day. They saw the image of Christ reflected in tears and blood, in the glorious company of the apostles, the goodly fellowship of the prophets, and the noble army of martyrs; they read in prophecy of the doom of the Church as "a woman fed by God in the wilderness" (see Rev. 12:6) and her witnesses as "clothed in sackcloth" (Rev. 11:3), and they could not believe that they were meant for nothing more than to enjoy the pleasures of this life, however innocent and moderate might be their use of them. Without deciding about their neighbors, they felt themselves called to higher things; their own sense of the duty became the sanction and witness of it. They considered that God, at least, would afflict them in His love if they spared themselves ever so much. The thorn in the flesh, the buffetings of Satan, the bereavement of their eyes — these were their portion; and, in common prudence, were there no higher thought they could not live out of time and measure with these expected visitations. With no superstitious alarms, or cowardly imaginations, or senseless hurrying into difficulty or trial, but calmly and in faith, they surrendered themselves into His hands, who had told them in His inspired word that affliction was to be their familiar food; till at length they gained such distaste for the luxuries of life as to be impatient of them from their very fullness of grace.

Even in these days, when the "fine gold has become dim" (Lam. 4:1), such has been the mind of those we most revere.[2] But such was it especially in primitive times. It was the temper, too, of those apostles who were removed, more than their brethren, from the world's buffetings, as if the prospect of suffering afterward were no ground of dispensation for a present self-inflicted discipline but rather demanded it. St. James the Less was Bishop of Jerusalem and was highly venerated for his uprightness by the unbelieving Jews among whom he lived unmolested. We are told that he drank no wine nor strong drink, nor did he eat any animal food nor indulge in the luxury of the bath. "So often was he in the Temple on his knees that they were thin and hard by his continual supplication" (Eusebius, *The Ecclesiastical History*, 2.23.6). Thus he kept his "loins girded about, and his lamp burning" for the blessed martyrdom that was to end his course (Luke 12:35). Could it be otherwise? How could the great apostle, sitting at home by his Lord's decree, "nourish his heart," as he calls it, "as for the slaughter" (James 5:5)? How could he eat and drink and live as other men when "the Ark, and Israel, and Judah were in tents" (2 Sam. 11:11), encamped in the open fields, and one by one God's chosen warriors were falling before the brief triumph of Satan! How could he be "delicate on the earth, and wanton" (James 5:5) when Paul and

---

[2]   "It is a most miserable state for a man to have everything according to his desire and quietly to enjoy the pleasures of life. There needs no more to expose him to eternal misery" (Bishop Wilson, *Sacra Privata*, "Wednesday").

Barnabas, Peter, too, and John were in stripes and prisons, in labors and perils, in hunger and thirst, in cold and nakedness! Stephen had led the army of martyrs in Jerusalem itself, which was his own post of service. James, the brother of John, had followed him in the same city; he first of the apostles tasting our Lord's cup who had unwittingly asked to drink it. And if this was the feeling of the apostles, when in temporary safety, why is it not ours who altogether live at ease, except that we have not faith enough to realize what is past? Could we see the Cross upon Calvary and the list of sufferers who resisted unto blood in the times that followed it, is it possible that we should feel surprise when pain overtook us, or impatience at its continuance? Is it strange though we are smitten by ever so new a plague? Is it grievous that the Cross presses on one nerve or limb ever so many years till hope of relief is gone? Is it, indeed, not possible with the apostle to rejoice in "bearing in our body the marks of the Lord Jesus" (Gal. 6:17)? And much more can we, for very shame's sake, suffer ourselves to be troubled at what is but ordinary pain, to be irritated or saddened, made gloomy or anxious by inconveniences that never could surprise or unsettle those who had studied and understood their place as servants of a crucified Lord?

Let us, then, determine with cheerful hearts to sacrifice unto the Lord our God our comforts and pleasures, however innocent, when He calls for them, whether for the purposes of His Church or in His own inscrutable Providence. Let us lend to Him a few short hours of present ease, and we shall receive our own with abundant usury in the day of His coming. There is a Treasury in Heaven stored with such offerings as the natural man abhors; with sighs and tears, wounds and blood, torture and death. The martyrs first began the contribution, and we all may follow them; all of us, for every suffering, great or little, may, like the widow's mite, be sacrificed in faith to

Him who sent it. Christ gave us the words of consecration when He for an ensample said, "Thy will be done" (Matt. 6:10). Henceforth, as the apostle speaks, we may "glory in tribulation" as the seed of future glory (Rom. 5:3).

Meanwhile, let us never forget in all we suffer that, properly speaking, our own sin is the cause of it, and it is only by Christ's mercy that we are allowed to range ourselves at His side. We who are children of wrath are made through Him children of grace; and our pains — which are in themselves but foretastes of Hell — are changed by the sprinkling of His blood into a preparation for Heaven.

Chapter 2

Mental Sufferings of Our Lord in His Passion

Every passage in the history of our Lord and Savior is of unfathomable depth and affords inexhaustible matter of contemplation. All that concerns Him is infinite, and what we first discern is but the surface of that which begins and ends in eternity. It would be presumptuous for anyone short of saints and doctors to attempt to comment on His words and deeds, except in the way of meditation; but meditation and mental prayer are so much a duty in all who wish to cherish true faith and love toward Him that it may be allowed us, my brethren, under the guidance of holy men who have gone before us, to dwell and enlarge upon what otherwise would more fitly be adored than scrutinized. And certain times of the year, Passiontide especially, call upon us to consider, as closely and minutely as we can, even the more sacred portions of the Gospel history. I would rather be thought feeble or officious in my treatment of them than wanting to the season; and so I now proceed, because the religious usage of the Church requires it, and though any individual preacher may well shrink from it, to direct your thoughts to a subject, especially suitable now, and about which many of us perhaps think very little: the sufferings that our Lord endured in His innocent and sinless soul.

You know, my brethren, that our Lord and Savior, though He was God, was also perfect man; and hence He had not only a body but a soul likewise, such as ours, though pure from all stain of evil. He did not take a body without a soul — God forbid! — for that would not have been to become man. How would He have sanctified our nature by taking a nature that was not ours? Man without a soul is on a level with the beasts of the field; but our Lord came to save a race capable of praising and obeying Him, possessed of immortality, though that immortality had lost its promised blessedness. Man was created in the image of God, and that image is in his soul; when then his Maker, by an unspeakable condescension, came in his nature, He took on Himself a soul in order to take on Him a body; He took on Him a soul as the means of His union with a body; He took on Him in the first place the soul then the body of man, both at once but in this order, the soul and the body; He Himself created the soul that He took on Himself, while He took His body from the flesh of the Blessed Virgin, His Mother. Thus He became perfect man with body and soul; and as He took on Him a body of flesh and nerves, which admitted of wounds and death and was capable of suffering, so did He take a soul, too, that was susceptible of that suffering, and moreover was susceptible of the pain and sorrow that are proper to a human soul; and, as His atoning Passion was undergone in the body, so it was undergone in the soul also.

As the solemn days proceed, we shall be especially called on, my brethren, to consider His sufferings in the body, His seizure, His forced journeyings to and fro, His blows and wounds, His scourging, the crown of thorns, the nails, the Cross. They are all summed up in the Crucifix itself as it meets our eyes; they are represented all at once on His sacred flesh as it hangs up before us — and meditation is made easy by the spectacle. It is otherwise with the sufferings of His soul; they cannot be painted for us, nor can they even be duly investigated: they are beyond both sense and thought, and yet they anticipated His bodily sufferings. The agony, a pain of the soul, not of the body, was the first act of His tremendous sacrifice: "My soul is sorrowful even unto death," He said (Matt. 26:38); nay; if He suffered in the body, it really was in the soul, for the body did but convey the infliction on to that which was the true recipient and seat of the suffering.

This it is very much to the purpose to insist upon: I say, it was not the body that suffered but the soul in the body; it was the soul and not the body that was the seat of the suffering of the Eternal Word. Consider, then, there is no real pain, though there may be apparent suffering, when there is no kind of inward sensibility or spirit to be the seat of it. A tree, for instance, has life, organs, growth, and decay; it may be wounded and injured; it droops, and it is killed; but it does not suffer, because it has no mind or sensible principle within it. But wherever this gift of an immaterial principle is found, there pain is possible, and greater pain according to the quality of the gift. Had we no spirit of any kind, we should feel as little as a tree feels; had we no soul, we should not feel pain more acutely than a brute feels it; but, being men, we feel pain in a way in which none but those who have souls can feel it.

Living beings, I say, feel more or less according to the spirit that is in them; brutes feel far less than man because they cannot reflect on what they feel; they have no advertence or direct consciousness of their sufferings. This it is that makes pain so trying, that is, that we cannot help thinking of it while we suffer it. It is before us, it possesses the mind, it keeps our thoughts fixed upon it. Whatever draws the mind off the thought of it lessens it; hence friends try to amuse us when we are in pain, for amusement is a diversion. If the pain is slight, they sometimes succeed with us; and then we are, so to say, without pain, even while we suffer. And hence it continually happens that in violent exercise or labor, men meet with blows or cuts, so considerable and so durable in their effect, as to bear witness to the suffering that must have attended their infliction, of which nevertheless they recollect nothing. And in quarrels and in battles wounds are received that, from the excitement of the moment, are brought home to the consciousness of the combatant not by the pain at the time of receiving them but by the loss of blood that follows.

I will show you presently, my brethren, how I mean to apply what I have said to the consideration of our Lord's sufferings; first I will make another remark. Consider, then, that hardly any one stroke of pain is intolerable; it is intolerable when it continues. You cry out perhaps that you cannot bear more; patients feel as if they could stop the surgeon's hand simply because he continues to pain them. Their feeling is that they have borne as much as they can bear, as if the continuance and not the intenseness was what made it too much for them. What does this mean but that the memory of the foregoing moments of pain acts upon and (as it were) edges the pain that succeeds? If the third or fourth or twentieth moment of pain could be taken by itself, if the succession of the moments that preceded it could be forgotten, it would be no more than the first moment, as bearable as the first (taking away the shock that accompanies the first); but what makes it unbearable is that it is the twentieth; that the first, the second, the third, on to the nineteenth moment of pain, are all concentrated in the twentieth; so that every additional moment of pain has all the force, the ever-increasing force, of all that has preceded it. Hence, I repeat, it is that brute animals would seem to feel so little pain because, that is, they have not the power of reflection or of consciousness. They do not know they exist; they do not contemplate themselves; they do not look backward or forward; every moment as it succeeds is their all; they wander over the face of the earth and see this thing and that, and they feel pleasure and pain, but still they take everything as it comes and then let it go again, as men do in dreams. They have memory but not the memory of an intellectual being; they put together nothing, they make nothing properly one and individual to themselves out of the particular sensations that they receive; nothing is to them a reality or has a substance beyond those sensations; they are but sensible of a number of successive impressions. And hence, as their other feelings, so their feeling of pain is but faint and dull, in spite of their outward manifestations of it. It is the intellectual comprehension of pain, as a whole diffused through successive moments, that gives it its special power and keenness, and it is the soul only, which a brute has not, that is capable of that comprehension.

Now apply this to the sufferings of our Lord; do you recollect their offering Him wine mingled with myrrh when He was on the point of being crucified? He would not drink of it; why? Because such a portion would have stupefied His mind, and He was bent on bearing the pain in all its bitterness. You see from this, my brethren, the character of His sufferings; He would have fain escaped them had that been His Father's will: "If it be possible," He said, "let this chalice pass from Me" (Matt. 26:39), but since it was not possible, He says calmly and decidedly to the apostle who would have rescued Him from suffering, "The chalice which My Father hath given Me, shall I not drink it?" (John 18:11). If He was to suffer, He gave Himself to suffering; He did not come to suffer as little as He could; He did not turn away His face from the suffering; He confronted it, or, as I may say, He breasted it, that every particular portion of it might make its due impression on Him. And as men are superior to brute animals and are affected by pain more than they by reason of the mind within them, which gives a substance to pain such as it cannot have in the instance of brutes, so, in like manner, our Lord felt pain of the body with an advertence and a consciousness, and therefore with a keenness and intensity and with a unity of perception, that none of us can possibly fathom or compass because His soul was so absolutely in His power, so simply free from the influence of distractions, so fully directed upon the pain, so utterly surrendered, so simply subjected to the suffering. And thus He may truly be said to have suffered the whole of His Passion in every moment of it.

Recollect that our Blessed Lord was in this respect different from us: that though He was perfect man, yet there was a power in Him greater than His soul that ruled His soul, for He was God. The soul of other men is subjected to its own wishes, feelings, impulses, passions, perturbations; His soul was subjected simply to His eternal and divine personality. Nothing happened to His soul by chance or on a sudden; He never was taken by surprise; nothing affected Him without His willing beforehand that it should affect Him. Never did He sorrow, or fear, or desire, or rejoice in spirit but He first willed to be sorrowful, or afraid, or desirous, or joyful. When we suffer, it is because outward agents and the uncontrollable emotions of our minds bring suffering upon us. We are brought under the discipline of pain involuntarily, we suffer from it more or less acutely according to accidental circumstances, we find our patience more or less tried by it according to our state of mind, and we do our best to provide alleviations or remedies of it. We cannot anticipate beforehand how much of it will come upon us or how far we shall be able to sustain it; nor can we say afterward why we have felt just what we have felt or why we did not bear the suffering better. It was otherwise with our Lord. His Divine Person was not subject, could not be exposed, to the influence of His own human affections and feelings except so far as He chose. I repeat, when He chose to fear, He feared; when He chose to be angry, He was angry; when He chose to grieve, He was grieved. He was not open to emotion, but He opened upon Himself voluntarily the impulse by which He was moved. Consequently, when He determined to suffer the pain of His vicarious Passion, whatever He did, He did, as the wise man says, *instanter*, "earnestly," with His might; He did not do it by halves; He did not turn away His mind from the suffering as we do (how should He, who came to suffer, who could not have suffered but of His own act?). No, He did not say and unsay, do and undo; He said and He did; He said, "Lo, I come to do Thy will, O God; sacrifice and offering Thou wouldest not, but a body hast Thou fitted to Me" (Heb. 10:9, 5). He took a body in order that He might suffer; He became man that He might suffer as man; and when His hour was come, that hour of Satan and of darkness, the hour when sin was to pour its full malignity upon Him, it followed that He offered Himself wholly, a holocaust, a whole burnt offering: as the whole of His body stretched out upon the Cross, so the whole of His soul — His whole advertence, His whole consciousness, a mind awake, a sense acute, a living cooperation, a present, absolute intention, not a virtual permission, not a heartless submission — did He present to His tormentors. His Passion was an action; He lived most energetically while He lay languishing, fainting, and dying. Nor did He die except by an act of the will, for He bowed His head in command as well as in resignation and said, "Father, into Thy hands I commend My Spirit" (Luke 23:46); He gave the word, He surrendered His soul, He did not lose it.

Thus, you see, my brethren, had our Lord only suffered in the body, and in it not so much as other men, still as regards the pain, He would have really suffered indefinitely more, because pain is to be measured by the power of realizing it. God was the sufferer; God suffered in His human nature; the sufferings belonged to God and were drunk up, were drained out to the bottom of the chalice, because God drank them, not tasted or sipped, not flavored, disguised by human medicaments, as man disposes of the cup of anguish. And what I have been saying will further serve to answer an objection that I shall proceed to notice and that perhaps exists latently in the minds of many and leads them to overlook the part that our Lord's soul had in His gracious satisfaction for sin.

Our Lord said, when His agony was commencing, "My soul is sorrowful unto death"; now you may ask, my brethren, whether He had not certain consolations peculiar to Himself, impossible in any other, that diminished or impeded the distress of His soul and caused Him to feel not more but less than an ordinary man. For instance, He had a sense of innocence that no other sufferer could have; even His persecutors, even the false apostle who betrayed Him, the judge who sentenced Him, and the soldiers who conducted the execution, testified His innocence: "I have condemned the innocent blood," said Judas (Matt. 27:4); "I am clear from the blood of this just Person," said Pilate (Matt. 27:24); "Truly this was a just Man," cried the centurion (Luke 23:47). And if even they, sinners, bore witness to His sinlessness, how much more did His own soul! And we know well that even in our own case, sinners as we are, on the consciousness of innocence or of guilt mainly turns our power of enduring opposition and calumny; how much more, you will say, in the case of our Lord, did the sense of inward sanctity compensate for the suffering and annihilate the shame! Again, you may say that He knew that His sufferings would be short and that their issue would be joyful, whereas uncertainty of the future is the keenest element of human distress; but He could not have anxiety for He was not in suspense, nor despondency or despair for He never was deserted. And in confirmation you may refer to St. Paul, who expressly tells us that "for the joy set before Him," our Lord "despised the shame" (Heb. 12:2). And certainly there is a marvelous calm and self-possession in all He does: consider His warning to the apostles, "Watch and pray, lest ye enter into temptation; the spirit indeed is willing, but the flesh is weak" (Mark 14:38); or His words to Judas, "Friend, wherefore art thou come?" (Matt. 26:50), and "Judas, betrayest thou the Son of Man with a kiss?" (Luke 22:48); or to Peter, "All that take the sword shall perish with the sword" (Matt. 26:52); or to the man who struck Him, "If I have spoken evil, bear witness of the evil; but if well, why smitest thou Me?" (John 18:23); or to His Mother, "Woman, behold thy Son" (John 19:26).

All this is true and much to be insisted on, but it quite agrees with, or rather illustrates, what I have been observing. My brethren, you have only said (to use a human phrase) that He was always Himself. His mind was its own center and was never in the slightest degree thrown off its heavenly and most perfect balance. What He suffered, He suffered because He put Himself under suffering, and that deliberately and calmly. As He said to the leper, "I will, be thou clean" (Matt. 8:3); and to the paralytic, "Thy sins be forgiven thee" (Matt. 9:5; Luke 5:23); and to the centurion, "I will come and heal him" (Matt. 8:7); and of Lazarus, "I go to wake him out of sleep" (John 11:11); so He said, "Now I will begin to suffer," and He did begin. His composure is but the proof of how entirely He governed His own mind. He drew back, at the proper moment, the bolts and fastenings; He opened the gates, and the floods fell right upon His soul in all their fullness. That is what St. Mark tells us of Him, and he is said to have written his Gospel from the very mouth of St. Peter, who was one of three witnesses present at the time. "They came," he says, "to the place which is called Gethsemane; and He saith to His disciples, Sit you here while I pray. And He taketh with Him Peter and James and John, and He began to be frightened and to be very heavy" (Mark 14:32–33). You see how deliberately He acts; He comes to a certain spot, and then, giving the word of command and withdrawing the support of the Godhead from His soul, distress, terror, and dejection at once rush in upon it. Thus He walks forth into a mental agony with as definite an action as if it were some bodily torture, the fire or the wheel.

This being the case, you will see at once, my brethren, that it is nothing to the purpose to say that He would be supported under His trial by the consciousness of innocence and the anticipation of triumph; for His trial consisted in the withdrawal (as of other causes of consolation), so of that very consciousness and anticipation. The same act of the will that admitted the influence upon His soul of any distress at all admitted all distresses at once. It was not the contest between antagonist impulses and views coming from without, but the operation of an inward resolution. As men of self-command can turn from one thought to another at their will, so much more did He deliberately deny Himself the comfort and satiate Himself with the woe. In that moment, His soul thought not of the future: He thought only of the present burden that was upon Him and that He had come upon earth to sustain.

And now, my brethren, what was it He had to bear when He thus opened upon His soul the torrent of this predestinated pain? Alas! He had to bear what is well known to us, what is familiar to us, but what to Him was woe unutterable. He had to bear that which is so easy a thing to us, so natural, so welcome, that we cannot conceive of it as of a great endurance, but which to Him had the scent and the poison of death — He had, my dear brethren, to bear the weight of sin; He had to bear your sins; He had to bear the sins of the whole world. Sin is an easy thing to us; we think little of it; we do not understand how the Creator can think much of it; we cannot bring our imagination to believe that it deserves retribution, and, when even in this world punishments follow upon it, we explain them away or turn our minds from them. But consider what sin is in itself: it is rebellion against God; it is a traitor's act who aims at the overthrow and death of His sovereign; it is that, if I may use a strong expression, which, could the divine Governor of the world cease to be, would be sufficient to bring it about. Sin is the mortal enemy of the All-Holy, so that He and it cannot be together; and as the All-Holy drives it from His presence into the outer darkness, so, if God could be less than God, it is sin that would have power to make Him less. And here observe, my brethren, that when once Almighty Love, by taking flesh, entered this created system and submitted Himself to its laws, then forthwith this antagonist of good and truth, taking advantage of the opportunity, flew at that flesh that He had taken and fixed on it and was its death. The envy of the Pharisees, the treachery of Judas, and the madness of the people were but the instrument or the expression of the enmity that sin felt toward Eternal Purity as soon as, in infinite mercy toward men, He put Himself within its reach. Sin could not touch His divine majesty; but it could assail Him in that way in which He allowed Himself to be assailed, that is, through the medium of His humanity. And in the issue, in the death of God incarnate, you are but taught, my brethren, what sin is in itself and what it was that then was falling, in its hour and in its strength, upon His human nature, when He allowed that nature to be so filled with horror and dismay at the very anticipation.

There, then, in that most awful hour, knelt the Savior of the world, putting off the defenses of His divinity, dismissing His reluctant angels, who in myriads were ready at His call, and opening His arms, baring His breast, sinless as He was, to the assault of His foe — a foe whose breath was a pestilence and whose embrace was an agony. There He knelt, motionless and still, while the vile and horrible fiend clad His spirit in a robe steeped in all that is hateful and heinous in human crime, which clung close round His heart, and filled His conscience, and found its way into every sense and pore of

His mind, and spread over Him a moral leprosy, till He almost felt Himself to be that which He never could be and which His foe would fain have made Him. Oh, the horror when He looked and did not know Himself and felt as a foul and loathsome sinner from His vivid perception of that mass of corruption that poured over His head and ran down even to the skirts of His garments! Oh, the distraction when He found His eyes and hands and feet and lips and heart as if the members of the Evil One and not of God! Are these the hands of the Immaculate Lamb of God, once innocent, but now red with ten thousand barbarous deeds of blood? Are these His lips, not uttering prayer and praise and holy blessings, but as if defiled with oaths and blasphemies and doctrines of devils? Or His eyes, profaned as they are by all the evil visions and idolatrous fascinations for which men have abandoned their adorable Creator? And His ears, they ring with sounds of revelry and of strife; and His heart is frozen with avarice and cruelty and unbelief; and His very memory is laden with every sin that has been committed since the Fall, in all regions of the earth, with the pride of the old giants, and the lusts of the five cities, and the obduracy of Egypt, and the ambition of Babel, and the unthankfulness and scorn of Israel. Oh, who does not know the misery of a haunting thought that comes again and again in spite of rejection to annoy if it cannot seduce? Or of some odious and sickening imagination, in no sense one's own, but forced upon the mind from without? Or of evil knowledge, gained with or without a man's fault, but which he would give a great price to be rid of at once and for ever? And adversaries such as these gather around Thee, Blessed Lord, in millions now; they come in troops more numerous than the locust or the palmerworm, or the plagues of hail and flies and frogs that were sent against Pharaoh. Of the living and of the dead and of the as yet unborn, of the lost and of the saved, of Thy people and of strangers, of sinners and of saints — all sins are there. Thy dearest are there,

Thy saints and Thy chosen are upon Thee, Thy three apostles, Peter, James, and John, but not as comforters but as accusers, like the friends of Job, "sprinkling dust toward Heaven" and heaping curses on Thy head (Job 2:12). All are there but one; one only is not there, one only; for she who had no part in sin, she only could console Thee, and therefore she is not nigh. She will be near Thee on the Cross, she is separated from Thee in the garden. She has been Thy companion and Thy confidant through Thy life, she interchanged with Thee the pure thoughts and holy meditations of thirty years; but her virgin ear may not take in, nor may her immaculate heart conceive, what now is in vision before Thee. None was equal to the weight but God; sometimes before Thy saints Thou hast brought the image of a single sin as it appears in the light of Thy countenance, or of venial sins, not mortal; and they have told us that the sight did all but kill them, nay, would have killed them, had it not been instantly withdrawn. The Mother of God, for all her sanctity, nay by reason of it, could not have borne even one brood of that innumerable progeny of Satan that now compasses Thee about. It is the long history of a world, and God alone can bear the load of it. Hopes blighted, vows broken, lights quenched, warnings scorned, opportunities lost; the innocent betrayed, the young hardened, the penitent relapsing, the just overcome, the aged failing; the sophistry of misbelief, the willfulness of passion, the obduracy of pride, the tyranny of habit, the canker of remorse, the wasting fever of care, the anguish of shame, the pining of disappointment, the sickness of despair; such cruel, such pitiable spectacles, such heartrending, revolting, detestable, maddening scenes; nay, the haggard faces, the convulsed lips, the flushed cheek, the dark brow of the willing slaves of evil, they are all before Him now; they are upon Him and in Him. They are with Him instead of that ineffable peace that has inhabited His soul since the moment of His conception. They are upon Him; they are all but His own; He cries to His Father as if He were the criminal, not the victim; His agony takes the form of guilt and compunction. He is doing penance, He is making confession, He is exercising contrition with a reality and a virtue infinitely greater than that of all saints and penitents together; for He is the One Victim for us all, the sole Satisfaction, the real Penitent, all but the real sinner.

He rises languidly from the earth and turns around to meet the traitor and his band, now quickly nearing the deep shade. He turns, and lo there is blood upon His garment and in His footprints. Whence come these first fruits of the Passion of the Lamb? No soldier's scourge has touched His shoulders, nor the hangman's nails His hands and feet. My brethren, He has bled before His time; He has shed blood; yes, and it is His agonizing soul that has broken up His framework of flesh and poured it forth. His Passion has begun from within. That tormented Heart, the seat of tenderness and love, began at length to labor and to beat with vehemence beyond its nature; "the foundations of the great deep were broken up" (Gen. 7:11); the red streams rushed forth so copious and fierce as to overflow the veins, and bursting through the pores, they stood in a thick dew over His whole skin; then forming into drops, they rolled down full and heavy and drenched the ground.

"My soul is sorrowful even unto death," He said. It has been said of that dreadful pestilence that now is upon us, that it begins with death; by which is meant that it has no stage or crisis, that hope is over when it comes, and that what looks like its course is but the death agony and the process of dissolution; and thus our Atoning Sacrifice, in a much higher sense, began with this Passion of woe and only did not die because at His omnipotent will His heart did not break, nor soul separate from body, till He had suffered on the Cross.

No; He has not yet exhausted that full chalice from which at first His natural infirmity shrank. The seizure and the arraignment, and the buffeting, and the prison, and the trial, and the mocking, and the passing to and fro, and the scourging, and the crown of thorns, and the slow march to Calvary, and the Crucifixion — these are all to come. A night and a day, hour after hour, are slowly to run out before the end comes and the satisfaction is completed.

And then, when the appointed moment arrived and He gave the word, as His Passion had begun with His soul, with the soul did it end. He did not die of bodily exhaustion or of bodily pain; at His will His tormented Heart broke and He commended His Spirit to the Father.

> *O Heart of Jesus, all Love, I offer Thee these humble prayers for myself, and for all those who unite themselves with me in Spirit to adore Thee. O holiest Heart of Jesus most lovely, I intend to renew and to offer to Thee these acts of adoration and these prayers, for myself a wretched sinner, and for all those who are associated with me in Thy adoration, through all moments while I breathe, even to the end of my life. I recommend to Thee, O my Jesus, Holy Church, Thy dear spouse and our true Mother, all just souls and all poor sinners, the afflicted, the dying, and all mankind. Let not Thy Blood be shed for them in vain. Finally, deign to apply it in relief of the souls in Purgatory, of those in particular who have practiced in the course of their life this holy devotion of adoring Thee.*

Chapter 3

The Power of the Will

"Finally, my brethren, be strong in the Lord,
and in the power of His might."

Ephesians 6:10

Quinquagesima Sunday: The Last Sunday before Ash Wednesday

We know that there are great multitudes of professed Christians who, alas, have actually turned from God with a deliberate will and purpose and, in consequence, are at present strangers to the grace of God; though they do not know or do not care about this. But a vast number of Christians, half of the whole number at least, are in other circumstances. They have not thrown themselves out of a state of grace, nor have they to repent and turn to God in the sense in which those must who have allowed themselves in willful transgression, after the knowledge of the truth has been imparted to them. Numbers there are in all ranks of life who, having good parents and advisers, or safe homes, or religious pursuits, or being without strong feelings and passions, or for whatever reason, cannot be supposed to have put off from them the garment of divine grace and deserted to the ranks of the enemy. Yet are they not safe, nevertheless. It is plain, for surely it is not enough to avoid evil in order to attain to

Heaven; we must follow after good. What, then, is their danger? That of the unprofitable servant who hid his lord's money. As far removed as that slothful servant was from those who traded with their talents in his state and in his destiny, so far separate from one another are two classes of Christians who live together here as brethren — the one class is using grace, the other neglecting it; one is making progress, the other sitting still; one is working for a reward, the other is idle and worthless.

This view of things should ever be borne in mind when we speak of the state of grace. There are different degrees in which we may stand in God's favor; we may be rising or sinking in His favor; we may not have forfeited it, yet we may not be securing it; we may be safe for the present but have a dangerous prospect before us. We may be more or less "hypocrites," "slothful," "unprofitable," and yet our day of grace not be passed. We may still have the remains of our new nature lingering on us, the influences of grace present with us, and the power of amendment and conversion within us. We may still have talents that we may put to account and gifts that we may stir up. We may not be cast out of our state of justification and yet may be destitute of that love of God, love of God's truth, love of holiness, love of active and generous obedience, that honest surrender of self, that alone will secure to us hereafter the blessed words, "Well done, good and faithful servant: enter thou into the joy of thy Lord" (Matt. 25:21).

The only qualification that will avail us for Heaven is the love of God. We may keep from gross sinning and yet not have this divine gift without which we are dead in God's sight. This changes our whole being; this makes us live; this makes us grow in grace and abound in good works; this makes us fit for God's presence hereafter.

Now here I have said a number of things, each of which will bear drawing out by itself and insisting on.

No one can doubt that we are again and again exhorted in Scripture to be holy and perfect, to be holy and blameless in the sight of God, to be holy as He is holy, to keep the commandments, to fulfill the law, to be filled with the fruit of righteousness. Why do we not obey as we ought? Many people will answer that we have a fallen nature that hinders us; that we cannot help it, though we ought to be very sorry for it; that this is the reason of our shortcomings. Not so: we can help it; we are not hindered; what we want is the will; and it is our own fault that we have it not. We have all things granted to us; God has abounded in His mercies to us; we have a depth of power and strength lodged in us; but we have not the heart, we have not the will, we have not the love to use it. We lack this one thing, a desire to be newly made; and I think anyone who examines himself carefully will own that he does, and that this is the reason why he cannot and does not obey or make progress in holiness.

That we have this great gift within us, or are in a state of grace, for the two statements mean nearly the same thing, is very plain of course from Scripture. We all know what Scripture says on the subject, and yet even here it may be as well to dwell on one or two passages by way of reminding and impressing ourselves.

Consider then our Savior's words: "The water that I shall give him shall be in him a well of water springing up into everlasting life" (John 4:14). Exhaust the sea, it will not fill the infinite spaces of the heavens, but the gift within us may be drawn out till it fills eternity.

Again, consider St. Paul's most wonderful words in the Epistle from which the text is taken, when he gives glory to "Him who is able to do exceeding abundantly above all that we ask or think, according to the power that worketh in us" (Eph. 3:20). You observe here that there is a power given to us Christians that "worketh in us," a special, hidden, mysterious power that makes us its instruments. Even that we have souls is strange and mysterious. We do not see our souls, but we see in others and we are conscious in ourselves of a principle that rules our bodies and makes them what the brutes are not. We have that in us which informs our bodies and changes them from mere animal bodies into human. Brutes cannot talk; brutes have little expression of countenance; they cannot form into societies; they cannot progress. Why? Because they have not that hidden gift that we have — reason. Well, in like manner St. Paul speaks of Christians too as having a special power within them that they gain because they are, and when they become Christians; and he calls it, in the text to which I am referring, "the power that worketh in us." In a former chapter of the Epistle, he speaks of "the exceeding greatness of His power toward us who believe, according to the working of His mighty power" (Eph. 1:19); and he says that our eyes must be enlightened in order to recognize it; and he compares it to that divine power in Christ our Savior by which, working in due season, He was raised from the dead, so that the bonds of death had no dominion over Him. As seeds have life in them, which seem lifeless, so the Body of Christ had life in itself when it was dead; and so also, though not in a similar way, we too, sinners as we are, have a spiritual principle in us, if we did but exert it, so great, so wondrous, that all the powers in the visible world, all the conceivable forces and appetites of matter, all the physical miracles that are at this day in process of discovery, almost superseding time and space, dispensing with numbers, and rivaling mind, all these powers of nature are nothing to this gift within us. Why do I say this? Because the apostle tells us that God is able thereby "to do exceeding abundantly above all that we ask or think." You see, he labors for words to express the exuberant, overflowing fullness, the vast and unfathomable depth, or what he has just called "the breadth, and length, and depth, and height" of the gift given us (Eph. 3:18). And hence he elsewhere says, "I can do all things through Christ who strengtheneth me" (Phil. 4:13), where he uses the same word that occurs also in the text, "My brethren, be strong in the Lord, and in the power of His might" (Eph. 6:10). See what an accumulation of words! First, be strong or be ye made strong. Strong in what? Strong in power. In the power of what? In the power of His might, the might of God. Three words are used one on another to express the manifold gift that God has given us. He to might has added power, and power He has made grow into strength. We have the power of His might; nor only so, but the strength of the power of His might who is Almighty.

And this is the very account that St. Luke gives us of St. Paul's own state in the Book of Acts after his conversion. The Jews wondered, but "Saul increased the more in strength, and confounded the Jews who dwelt at Damascus" (Acts 9:22). He became more and more strong. And at the end of his course, when brought before the Romans, "The Lord," as he says, "stood with me, and strengthened me" (2 Tim. 4:17); and in turn he too exhorts Timothy, "Thou, therefore, my son, be strong in the grace that is in Christ Jesus; and the things that thou hast heard of me among many witnesses, the same commit thou to faithful men, who shall be able to teach others also. Thou therefore endure hardness, as a good soldier of Jesus Christ" (2 Tim. 2:1–3).

I said just now that we did not need Scripture to tell us of our divinely imparted power; that our own consciousness was sufficient. I do not mean to say that our consciousness will enable us to rise to the fullness of the apostle's expressions; for trial, of course, cannot ascertain an inexhaustible gift. All we can know of it by experience is that it goes beyond us, that we have never fathomed it, that we have drawn from it and never emptied it; that we have evidence that there is a power with us, how great we know not, that does for us what we cannot do for ourselves and is always equal to all our needs. And of as much as this, I think, we have abundant evidence.

Let us ask ourselves, why is it that we so often wish to do right and cannot? Why is it that we are so frail, feeble, languid, wayward, dim-sighted, fluctuating, perverse? Why is it that we cannot "do the things that we would" (Rom. 7:15–20). Why is it that, day after day, we remain irresolute, that we serve God so poorly, that we govern ourselves so weakly and so variably, that we cannot command our thoughts, that we are so slothful, so cowardly, so discontented, so sensual, so ignorant? Why is it that we, who trust that we are not by willful sin thrown out of grace (for of such I am all along speaking); why is it that we, who are ruled by no evil masters and bent upon no earthly ends, who are not covetous, or profligate livers, or worldly-minded, or ambitious, or envious, or proud, or unforgiving, or desirous of name; why is it that we, in the very kingdom of grace, surrounded by angels and preceded by saints, nevertheless can do so little, and instead of mounting with wings like eagles, grovel in the dust and do but sin and confess sin alternately? Is it that the power of God is not within us? Is it literally that we are not able to perform God's commandments? God forbid! We are able. We have that given us that makes us able. We are not in a state of nature. We have had the gift of grace implanted in us. We have a power within us to do what we are commanded to do. What is it we lack? The power? No; the will. What we lack is the real, simple, earnest, sincere inclination and aim to use what God has given us and what we have in us. I say, our experience tells us this. It is no matter of mere doctrine, much less a matter of words, but of things; a very practical, plain matter.

To take an instance of the simple kind. Is not the power to use our limbs our own, nay, even by nature? What, then, is sloth but a want of will? When we are not set on an object so greatly as to overcome the inconvenience of an effort, we remain as we are; when we ought to exert ourselves, we are slothful. But is the effort any effort at all when we desire that which needs the effort?

In like manner, to take a greater thing. Are not the feelings as distinct as well can be between remorse and repentance? In both a man is very sorry and ashamed of what he has done; in both he has a painful foreboding that he may perchance sin again in spite of his present grief. You will hear a man perhaps lament that he is so weak that he quite dreads what is to come another time, after all his good resolutions. There are cases, doubtless, in which a man is thus weak in power, though earnest in will; and, of course, it continually happens that he has ungovernable feelings and passions in spite of his better nature. But in a very great multitude of cases, this pretense of want of power is really but a want of will. When a man complains that he is under the dominion of any bad habit, let him seriously ask himself whether he has ever willed to get rid of it. Can he, with a simple mind, say in God's sight, "I wish it removed?"

A man, for instance, cannot attend to his prayers; his mind wanders; other thoughts intrude; time after time passes, and it is the same. Shall we say this arises from want of power? Of course it may be so; but before he says so, let him consider whether he has ever roused himself, shaken himself, awakened himself, got himself to will, if I may so say, attention. We know the feeling in unpleasant dreams, when we say to ourselves, "This is a dream," and yet cannot exert ourselves to will to be free from it; and how at length by an effort we will to move, and the spell at once is broken; we wake. So it is with sloth and indolence; the Evil One lies heavy on us, but he has no power over us except in our unwillingness to get rid of him. He cannot battle with us; he flies; he can do no more as soon as we propose to fight with him.

There is a famous instance of a holy man of old time who, before his conversion, felt indeed the excellence of purity but could not get himself to say more in prayer than "Give me chastity, but not yet." I will not be inconsiderate enough to make light of the power of temptation of any kind, nor will I presume to say that Almighty God will certainly shield a man from temptation for his wishing it; but whenever men complain, as they often do, of the arduousness of a high virtue, at least it were well that they should first ask themselves the question whether they desire to have it. We hear much in this day of the impossibility of heavenly purity — far be it from me to say that everyone has not his proper gift from God, one after this manner another after that — but O ye men of the world, when ye talk, as ye do, so much of the impossibility of this or that supernatural grace, when you disbelieve in the existence of severe self-rule, when you scoff at holy resolutions and affix a slur on those who make them, are you sure that the impossibility that you insist upon does not lie not in nature but in the will? Let us but will, and our nature is changed "according to the power that worketh in us." Say not, in excuse for others or for yourselves, that you cannot be other than Adam made you; you have never brought yourselves to will it — you cannot bear to will it. You cannot bear to be other than you are. Life would seem a blank to you were you other; yet what you are from not desiring a gift, this you make an excuse for not possessing it.

Let us take what trial we please — the world's ridicule or censure, loss of prospects, loss of admirers or friends, loss of ease, endurance of bodily pain — and recollect how easy our course has been directly we had once made up our mind to submit to it; how simple all that remained became, how wonderfully difficulties were removed from without, and how the soul was strengthened inwardly to do what was to be done. But it is seldom we have heart to throw ourselves, if I may so speak, on the Divine Arm; we dare not trust ourselves on the waters, though Christ bids us. We have not St. Peter's love to ask leave to come to Him upon the sea. When we once are filled with that heavenly charity, we can do all things because we attempt all things — for to attempt is to do.

I would have everyone carefully consider whether he has ever found God fail him in trial, when his own heart had not failed him; and whether he has not found strength greater and greater given him according to his day; whether he has not gained clear proof on trial that he has a divine power lodged within him and a certain conviction withal that he has not made the extreme trial of it or reached its limits. Grace ever outstrips prayer. Abraham ceased interceding ere God stayed from granting. Joash smote upon the ground but thrice when he might have gained five victories or six. All have the gift, many do not use it at all, none expend it. One wraps it in a napkin, another gains five pounds, another ten. It will bear thirty-fold, or sixty, or a hundred. We know not what we are or might be. As the seed has a tree within it, so men have within them angels.

Hence the great stress laid in Scripture on growing in grace. Seeds are intended to grow into trees. We are regenerated in order that we may be renewed daily after the Image of Him who has regenerated us. In the text and verses following, we have our calling set forth in order to "stir up our pure minds by way of remembrance" to the pursuit of it (2 Pet. 3:1). "Be strong in the Lord," says the apostle, "and in the power of His might. Put on the whole armor of God," with your loins girt about with truth, the breastplate of righteousness, your feet shod with the preparation of the gospel of peace, the shield of faith, the helmet of salvation, the sword of the Spirit (Eph. 6:10–18). One grace and then another is to be perfected in us. Each day is to bring forth its own treasure, till we stand, like blessed spirits, able and waiting to do the will of God.

Still more apposite are St. Peter's words, which go through the whole doctrine that I have been insisting on point by point. First, he tells us that "divine power hath given unto us all things that pertain unto life and godliness" (2 Pet. 1:3); that is, we have the gift. Then he speaks of the object that the gift is to effect, "exceeding great and precious promises are given unto us, that by these we may be partakers of the divine nature," that we who, by birth, are children of wrath, should become inwardly and really sons of God; putting off our former selves, or, as he says, "having escaped the corruption that is in the world through lust" (2 Pet. 1:4); that is, cleansing ourselves from all that remains in us of Original Sin, the infection of concupiscence. With which closely agree St. Paul's words to the Corinthians, "Having these promises," he says, "dearly beloved, let us cleanse ourselves from all defilement of the flesh and spirit, perfecting holiness in the fear of God" (2 Cor. 7:1). But to continue with St. Peter, "Giving all diligence," he says, "add to your faith virtue, and to virtue knowledge, and to knowledge temperance, and to temperance patience, and to patience godliness, and to godliness brotherly kindness, and to brotherly kindness charity" (2 Pet. 1:5–7). Next he speaks of those who, though they cannot be said to have forfeited God's grace, yet by a sluggish will and a lukewarm love have become but unprofitable, and "cumber the ground" in the Lord's vineyard: "He that lacketh these things is blind, and cannot see afar off, and hath forgotten that he was purged from his old sins" (2 Pet. 1:9); he has forgotten that cleansing that he once received when he was brought into the kingdom of grace. "Wherefore the rather, brethren, give diligence to make your calling and election sure; for if ye do these things, ye shall never fall; for so an entrance shall be ministered unto you abundantly, into the everlasting kingdom of our Lord and Savior Jesus Christ" (2 Pet. 1:10–11). Day by day shall ye enter deeper and deeper into the fullness of the riches of that kingdom, of which ye are made members.

Or, lastly, consider St. Paul's account of the same growth, and of the course of it, in his Epistle to the Romans: "Tribulation worketh patience, and patience experience, and experience hope, and hope maketh not ashamed." Such is the series of gifts, patience, experience, hope, a soul without shame — and whence all this? He continues, "because the love of God is shed abroad in our hearts, by the Holy Ghost which is given unto us" (Rom. 5:3–5).

Love can do all things; "charity never faileth" (1 Cor. 13:8); he who has the will has the power. You will say, "But is not the will itself from God? And, therefore, is it not after all His doing, not ours, if we have not the will?" Doubtless, by nature, our will is in bondage; we cannot will good; but by the grace of God our will has been set free; we obtain again, to a certain extent, the gift of free will; henceforth, we can will or not will. If we will, it is doubtless from God's grace, who gave us the power to will, and to Him be the praise; but it is from ourselves too, because we have used that power that God gave. God enables us to will and to do; by nature we cannot will, but by grace we can; and now if we do not will, we are the cause of the defect. What can Almighty Mercy do for us that He hath not done? "He has given all things which pertain to life and godliness;" and we, in consequence, can "make our calling and election sure" (2 Pet. 1:3, 10), as the holy men of God did of old time. Ah, how do those ancient saints put us to shame! How they were "out of weakness made strong," how they "waxed valiant in fight" and became as angels upon earth instead of men (Heb. 11:34)! And why? Because they had a heart to contemplate, to design, to will great things. Doubtless, in many respects, we all are but men to the end; we hunger, we thirst, we need sustenance, we need sleep, we need society, we need instruction, we need encouragement, we need example; yet who can say the heights to which in time men can proceed in all things, who beginning by little and little, yet in the distance shadow forth great things?

Enlarge the place of thy tent, and let them stretch forth the curtains of thine habitations; spare not, lengthen thy cords, and strengthen thy stakes; for thou shalt break forth on the right hand and on the left.... Fear not; for thou shalt not be ashamed; neither shalt thou be confounded, for thou shalt not be put to shame.... In righteousness shalt thou be established; thou shalt be far from oppression, for thou shalt not fear; and from terror, for it shall not come near thee.... This is the heritage of the servants of the Lord, and their righteousness is of Me, saith the Lord. (Isa. 54:2–4, 14, 17)

High words like these relate in the first place to the Church, but doubtless they are also fulfilled in their measure in each of her true children. But we sit coldly and sluggishly at home; we fold our hands and cry "a little more slumber;" we shut our eyes, we cannot see things afar off, we cannot "see the land which is very far off" (Isa. 33:17); we do not understand that Christ calls us after Him; we do not hear the voice of His heralds in the wilderness; we have not the heart to go forth to Him who multiplies the loaves and feeds us by every word of His mouth. Other children of Adam have before now done in His strength what we put aside. We fear to be too holy. Others put us to shame; all around us, others are doing what we will not. Others are entering deeper into the Kingdom of Heaven than we. Others are fighting against their enemies more truly and bravely. The unlettered, the ungifted, the young, the weak and simple, with sling and stones from the brook, are encountering Goliath as having on divine armor. The Church is rising up around us day by day toward Heaven, and we do nothing but object, or explain away, or criticize, or make excuses, or wonder. We fear to cast in our lot with the saints, lest we become a party; we fear to seek the strait gate, lest we be of the few not the many. Oh may we be loyal and affectionate before our race is run! Before our sun goes down in the grave, oh may we learn somewhat more of what the apostle calls the "love of Christ which passeth knowledge" (Eph. 3:19) and catch some of the rays of love that come from Him! Especially at the season of the year now approaching, when Christ calls us into the wilderness, let us gird up our loins and fearlessly obey the summons. Let us take up our cross and follow Him. Let us take to us "the whole armor of God, that we may be able to stand against the wiles of the devil; for we wrestle not against flesh and blood, but against principalities, against powers, against the rulers of the darkness of this world, against spiritual wickedness in high places; wherefore, take unto you the whole armor of God, that ye may be able to withstand in the evil day, and, having done all, to stand" (Eph. 6:11–13).

Chapter 4

Fasting: A Source of Trial

"And when He had fasted forty days and
forty nights, afterward He was hungry."

Matthew 4:2

First Sunday in Lent

The season of humiliation, which precedes Easter, lasts for forty days, in memory of our Lord's long fast in the wilderness. Accordingly, on this day, the first Sunday in Lent, we read the Gospel that gives an account of it, and in the Collect we pray Him, who for our sakes fasted forty days and forty nights, to bless our abstinence to the good of our souls and bodies.

We fast by way of penitence and in order to subdue the flesh. Our Savior had no need of fasting for either purpose. His fasting was unlike ours as in its intensity, so in its object. And yet when we begin to fast, His pattern is set before us; and we continue the time of fasting till, in number of days, we have equaled His.

There is a reason for this: in truth, we must do nothing except with Him in our eye. As He it is through whom alone we have the power to do any good thing, so unless we do it for Him, it is not good. From Him our obedience comes, toward Him it must look. He says, "Without Me ye can do nothing" (John 15:5). No work is good without grace and without love.

St. Paul gave up all things "to be found in Christ, not having mine own righteousness, which is of the law, but the righteousness which is from God upon faith" (Phil. 3:9). Then only are our righteousnesses acceptable when they are done not in a legal way but in Christ through faith. Vain were all the deeds of the Law because they were not attended by the power of the Spirit. They were the mere attempts of unaided nature to fulfill what it ought indeed but was not able to fulfill. None but the blind and carnal, or those who were in utter ignorance, could find aught in them to rejoice in. What were all the righteousnesses of the Law, what its deeds, even when more than ordinary, its alms and fastings, its disfiguring of faces and afflicting of souls; what was all this but dust and dross, a pitiful earthly service, a miserable hopeless penance, so far as the grace and the presence of Christ were absent? The Jews might humble themselves, but they did not rise in the spirit while they fell down in the flesh; they might afflict themselves, but it did not turn to their salvation; they might sorrow, but not as always rejoicing; the outward man might perish, but the inward man was not renewed day by day. They had the burden and heat of the day and the yoke of the Law, but it did not work out for them "a far more exceeding and eternal weight of glory" (2 Cor. 4:17). But God hath reserved some better thing for us. This is what it is to be one of Christ's little ones — to be able to do what the Jews thought they could do and could not; to have that within us through which we can do all things; to be possessed by His presence as our life, our strength, our merit, our hope, our crown; to become in a wonderful way His members, the instruments, or visible form, or sacramental sign, of the One Invisible Ever-Present Son of God, mystically reiterating in each of us all the acts of His earthly life, His birth, consecration, fasting, temptation, conflicts, victories, sufferings, agony, Passion, death, Resurrection, and Ascension; He being All in All, we, with as little power in ourselves, as little excellence or merit, as the water in Baptism or the bread and wine in Holy Communion; yet strong in the Lord and in the power of His might. These are the thoughts with which we celebrated Christmas and Epiphany; these are the thoughts that must accompany us through Lent.

Yes, even in our penitential exercises, when we could least have hoped to find a pattern in Him, Christ has gone before us to sanctify them to us. He has blessed fasting as a means of grace in that He has fasted; and fasting is only acceptable when it is done for His sake. Penitence is mere formality, or mere remorse, unless done in love. If we fast without uniting ourselves in heart to Christ — imitating Him and praying that He would make our fasting His own, would associate it with His own, and communicate to it the virtue of His own, so that we may be in Him, and He in us — we fast as Jews, not as Christians. Well, then, in the Services of this first Sunday, do we place the thought of Him before us whose grace must be within us, lest in our chastisements we beat the air and humble ourselves in vain.

Now in many ways the example of Christ may be made a comfort and encouragement to us at this season of the year.

And first of all, it will be well to insist on the circumstance that our Lord did thus retire from the world, as confirming to us the like duty, as far as we can observe it. This He did specially in the instance before us, before His entering upon His own ministry; but it is not the only instance recorded. Before He chose His apostles, He observed the same preparation. "It came to pass in those days that He went out into a mountain to pray, and continued all night in prayer to God" (Luke 6:12). Prayer through the night was a self-chastisement of the same kind as fasting. On another occasion, after sending away the multitudes, "He went up into a mountain apart to pray" (Matt. 14:23); and on this occasion also, He seems to have remained there through a great part of the night. Again, amid the excitement caused by His miracles, "In the morning, rising up a great while before day, He went out and departed into a solitary place, and there prayed" (Mark 1:35). Considering that our Lord is the pattern of human nature in its perfection, surely we cannot doubt that such instances of strict devotion are intended for our imitation, if we would be perfect. But the duty is placed beyond doubt by finding similar instances in the case of the most eminent of His servants. St. Paul, in the Epistle for this day, mentions among other sufferings that he and his brethren were "in watchings, in fastings" (2 Cor. 6:5), and in a later chapter, that he was "in fastings often" (2 Cor. 11:27). St. Peter retired to Joppa, to the house of one Simon, a tanner, on the seashore, and there fasted and prayed. Moses and Elijah both were supported through miraculous fasts, of the same length as our Lord's. Moses, indeed, at two separate times; as he tells us himself, "I fell down before the Lord, as at the first, forty days and forty nights; I did neither eat bread, nor drink water" (Deut. 9:18). Elijah, having been fed by an angel, "went in the strength of that meat forty days and forty nights" (1 Kings 19:8). Daniel "set his face unto the Lord his God, to seek by prayer and supplications, with fasting, and sackcloth, and ashes" (Dan. 9:3). Again, at another time, he says, "In those days, I, Daniel, was mourning three full weeks. I ate no pleasant bread, neither came flesh nor wine in my mouth, neither did I anoint myself at all, till three whole weeks were fulfilled" (Dan. 10:2–3). These are instances of fastings after the similitude of Christ.

Next, I observe that our Savior's fast was but introductory to His temptation. He went into the wilderness to be tempted of the devil, but before He was tempted, He fasted. Nor, as is worth notice, was this a mere preparation for the conflict, but it was the cause of the conflict in good measure. Instead of its simply arming Him against temptation, it is plain that in the first instance, His retirement and abstinence exposed Him to it. Fasting was the primary occasion of it. "When He had fasted forty days and forty nights, afterward He was hungry" (Matt. 4:2); and then the tempter came, bidding Him turn the stones into bread. Satan made use of His fast against Himself.

And this is singularly the case with Christians now who endeavor to imitate Him; and it is well they should know it, for else they will be discouraged when they practice abstinences. It is commonly said that fasting is intended to make us better Christians, to sober us and to bring us more entirely at Christ's feet in faith and humility. This is true, viewing matters on the whole. On the whole, and at last, this effect will be produced, but it is not at all certain that it will follow at once. On the contrary, such mortifications have at the time very various effects on different persons and are to be observed not from their visible benefits but from faith in the Word of God. Some men, indeed, are subdued by fasting and brought at once nearer to God; but others find it, however slight, scarcely more than an occasion of temptation. For instance, it is sometimes even made an objection to fasting, as if it were a reason for not practicing it, that it makes a man irritable and ill-tempered. I confess it often may do this. Again, what very often follows from it is a feebleness that deprives him of his command over his bodily acts, feelings, and expressions. Thus it makes him seem, for instance, to be out of temper when he is not; I mean, because his tongue, his lips, nay his brain, are not in his power. He does not use the words he wishes to use, nor the accent and tone. He seems sharp when he is not; and the consciousness of this and the reaction of that consciousness upon his mind is a temptation and actually makes him irritable, particularly if people misunderstand him and think him what he is not. Again, weakness of body may deprive him of self-command in other ways; perhaps he cannot help smiling or laughing when he ought to be serious, which is evidently a most distressing and humbling trial; or when wrong thoughts present themselves, his mind cannot throw them off, any more than if it were some dead thing and not spirit; but they then make an impression on him that he is not able to resist. Or again, weakness of body often hinders him from fixing his mind on his prayers, instead of making him pray more fervently; or again, weakness of body is often attended with languor and listlessness and strongly tempts a man to sloth. Yet I have not mentioned the most distressing of the effects that may follow from even the moderate exercise of this great Christian duty. It is undeniably a means of temptation, and I say so, lest persons should be surprised and despond when they find it so. And the merciful Lord knows that so it is from experience; and that He has experienced and thus knows it, as Scripture records, is to us a thought full of comfort. I do not mean to say, God forbid, that aught of sinful infirmity sullied His immaculate soul; but it is plain from the sacred history that in His case, as in ours, fasting opened the way to temptation. And perhaps this is the truest view of such exercises, that in some wonderful unknown way they open the next world for good and evil upon us and are an introduction to somewhat of an extraordinary conflict with the powers of evil. Stories are afloat (whether themselves true or not matters not, they show what the voice of mankind thinks *likely* to be true) of hermits in deserts being assaulted by Satan in strange ways, yet resisting the evil one and chasing him away, after our Lord's pattern and in His strength; and, I suppose, if we knew the secret history of men's minds in any age, we should find *this* (at least, I think I am not theorizing), that is, a remarkable union in the case of those who by God's grace have made advances in holy things (whatever be the case where men have not), a union on the one hand of temptations offered to the mind and, on the other, of the mind's not being affected by them, not consenting to them, even in momentary acts of the will, but simply hating them and receiving no harm from them. At least, I can conceive this — and so far, persons are evidently brought into fellowship and conformity with Christ's temptation, who was tempted yet without sin.

Let it not, then, distress Christians even if they find themselves exposed to thoughts from which they turn with abhorrence and terror. Rather let such a trial bring before their thoughts, with something of vividness and distinctness, the condescension of the Son of God. For if it be a trial to us creatures and sinners to have thoughts alien from our hearts presented to us, what must have been the suffering to the Eternal Word, God of God, and Light of Light, Holy and True, to have been so subjected to Satan that he could inflict every misery on Him short of sinning? Certainly it is a trial to us to have motives and feelings imputed to us before men by the accuser of the brethren that we never entertained; it is a trial to have ideas secretly suggested within from which we shrink; it is a trial to us for Satan to be allowed so to mix his own thoughts with ours that we feel guilty even when we are not; nay, to be able to set on fire our irrational nature, till in some sense we really sin against our will — but has not One gone before us more awful in His trial, more glorious in His victory? He was tempted in all points, "like as we are, yet without sin" (Heb. 4:15). Surely here, too, Christ's temptation speaks comfort and encouragement to us.

This then is, perhaps, a truer view of the consequences of fasting than is commonly taken. Of course, it is always, under God's grace, a spiritual benefit to our hearts eventually and improves them, through Him who worketh all in all; and it often is a sensible benefit to us at the time. Still it is often otherwise; often it but increases the excitability and susceptibility of our hearts; in all cases, it is therefore to be viewed chiefly as an *approach to God* — an approach to the powers of Heaven — yes, and to the powers of Hell.

And in this point of view there is something very awful in it. For what we know, Christ's temptation is but the fullness of that which, in its degree and according to our infirmities and corruptions, takes place in all His servants who seek Him. And if so, this surely was a strong reason for the Church's associating our season of humiliation with Christ's sojourn in the wilderness, that we might not be left to our own thoughts and, as it were, "with the wild beasts" (Mark 1:13), and thereupon despond when we afflict ourselves; but we might feel that we are what we really are, not bondmen of Satan and children of wrath, hopelessly groaning under our burden, confessing it, and crying out, "O wretched man!" but sinners indeed, and sinners afflicting themselves and doing penance for sin; but withal God's children, in whom repentance is fruitful, and who while they abase themselves are exalted, and at the very time that they are throwing themselves at the foot of the Cross, are still Christ's soldiers, sword in hand, fighting a generous warfare, and knowing that they have that in them, and upon them, that devils tremble at and flee.

And this is another point that calls for distinct notice in the history of our Savior's fasting and temptation, that is, the victory that attended it. He had three temptations, and thrice He conquered; at the last He said, "Get thee behind Me, Satan;" on which "the devil leaveth Him" (Matt. 4:10–11). This conflict and victory in the world unseen is intimated in other passages of Scripture. The most remarkable of these is what our Lord says with reference to the demoniac whom His apostles could not cure. He had just descended from the Mount of Transfiguration, where, let it be observed, He seems to have gone up with His favored apostles to pass the night in prayer. He came down after that communion with the unseen world and cast out the unclean spirit, and then He said, "This kind can come forth by nothing but by prayer and fasting" (Mark 9:29), which is nothing less than a plain declaration that such exercises give the soul power over the unseen world; nor can any sufficient reason be assigned for confining it to the first ages of the Gospel. And I think there is enough evidence, even in what may be known afterward of the effects of such exercises upon persons now (not to have recourse to history), to show that these exercises are God's instruments for giving the Christian a high and royal power above and over his fellows.

And since prayer is not only the weapon, ever necessary and sure, in our conflict with the powers of evil, but a deliverance from evil is ever implied as the object of prayer, it follows that all texts whatever that speak of our addressing and prevailing on Almighty God with prayer and fasting do, in fact, declare this conflict and promise this victory over the evil one. Thus in the parable, the importunate widow, who represents the Church in prayer, is not only earnest *with* God but *against* her adversary. "Avenge me of mine adversary," she says (Luke 18:3); and our "adversary" is "the devil," who, "as a roaring lion, walketh about seeking whom he may devour: whom resist," adds St. Peter, "steadfast in the faith" (1 Pet. 5:8–9). Let it be observed that, in this parable, *perseverance* in prayer is especially recommended to us. And this is part of the lesson taught us by the long continuance of the Lent fast — that we are not to gain our wishes by one day set apart for humiliation, or by one prayer, however fervent, but by "continuing instant in prayer" (Rom. 12:12). This too is signified to us in the account of Jacob's conflict. He, like our Savior, was occupied in it *through* the night. Who it was whom he was permitted to meet in that solitary season, we are not told; but He with whom he wrestled gave him strength to wrestle and at last left a token on him as if to show that he had prevailed only by the condescension of Him over whom he prevailed. So strengthened, he persevered till the morning broke and asked a blessing; and He whom he asked did bless him, giving him a new name in memory of his success. "Thy name shall be called no more Jacob, but Israel; for as a prince hast thou power with God and with men, and hast prevailed" (Gen. 32:28). In like manner, Moses passed one of his forty days' fast in confession and intercession for the people who had raised the golden calf. "Thus I fell down before the Lord forty days and forty nights, as I fell down at the first; because the Lord had said He would destroy you. I prayed therefore unto the Lord, and said, O Lord God, destroy not Thy people and Thine inheritance, which Thou hast redeemed through Thy greatness, which Thou hast brought forth out of Egypt with a mighty hand" (Deut. 9:25–26). Again, both of Daniel's recorded fasts ended in a blessing. His first was intercessory for his people, and the prophecy of the seventy weeks was given him. The second was also rewarded with prophetical disclosures; and what is remarkable, it seems to have had an influence (if I may use such a word) upon the unseen world from the time he began it: "The angel said, Fear not, Daniel, for *from the first day* that thou didst set thine heart to understand, and to chasten thyself before thy God, thy words were heard, and *I am come* for thy words" (Dan. 10:12). He came at the end, but he prepared to go at the beginning. But more than this, the angel proceeds, "But the prince of the kingdom of Persia withstood me one and twenty days," just the time during which Daniel had been praying, "but lo, Michael, one of the chief princes, came to help me, and I remained there with the kings of Persia" (Dan. 10:13).

An angel came to Daniel upon his fast; so too in our Lord's instance, angels came and ministered unto Him; and so we too may well believe, and take comfort in the thought, that even now, angels are especially sent to those who thus seek God. Not Daniel only, but Elijah too was, during his fast, strengthened by an angel; an angel appeared to Cornelius, while he was fasting and in prayer; and I do really think that there is enough in what religious persons may see around them to serve to confirm this hope thus gathered from the word of God.

"He shall give His angels charge over Thee, to keep Thee in all Thy ways" (Ps. 91:11), and the devil knows of this promise, for he used it in that very hour of temptation. He knows full well what our power is and what is his own weakness. So we have nothing to fear while we remain within the shadow of the throne of the Almighty: "A thousand shall fall beside Thee, and ten thousand at Thy right hand, but it shall not come nigh Thee" (Ps. 91:7). While we are found in Christ, we are partakers of His security. He has broken the power of Satan; He has gone "upon the lion and adder, the young lion and the dragon hath He trod under His feet" (Ps. 91:13); and henceforth evil spirits, instead of having power over us, tremble and are affrighted at every true Christian. They know he has that in him that makes him their master; that he may, if he will, laugh them to scorn and put them to flight. They know this well and bear it in mind in all their assaults upon him; sin alone gives them power over him; and their great object is to make him sin and therefore to surprise him into sin, knowing they have no other way of overcoming him. They try to scare him by the appearance of danger, and so to surprise him; or they approach stealthily and covertly to seduce him, and so to surprise him. But except by taking him at unawares, they can do nothing. Therefore let us be, my brethren, "not ignorant of his devices" (2 Cor. 2:11), and as knowing them, let us watch, fast, and pray; let us keep close under the wings of the Almighty, that He may be our shield and buckler. Let us pray Him to make known to us His will, to teach us our faults, to take from us whatever may offend Him, and to lead us in the way everlasting. And during this sacred season, let us look upon ourselves as on the Mount with Him — within the veil, hid with Him, not out of Him or apart from Him, in whose presence alone is life, but with and in

Him — learning of His Law with Moses, of His attributes with Elijah, of His counsels with Daniel, learning to repent, learning to confess and to amend, learning His love and His fear, unlearning ourselves, and growing up unto Him who is our Head.

C H A P T E R 5

Life: The Season of Repentance

"And when Esau heard the words of his father, he cried
with a great and exceeding bitter cry, and said unto
his father, Bless me, even me also, O my father."

Genesis 27:34

Second Sunday in Lent

I suppose no one can read this chapter without feeling some pity
for Esau. He had expected that his father would give him his blessing,
but his brother was beforehand with him and got the blessing instead.
He did not know what had happened, and he came in to his father to
be blessed without any suspicion that he was not to be blessed. His
father, full of amazement and distress, told him that without knowing
it, for he was blind and could not see, he had already given the blessing
to his brother Jacob, and he could not recall it. On hearing this, Esau
burst out into "a great and exceeding bitter cry," as the text expresses
it. All his hopes were disappointed in a moment. He had built much
upon this blessing. For Esau, when he was young, had committed a
very great sin against God. He was his father's firstborn, and in those
times, as now among the rich and noble, it was a great thing to be the
eldest in a family. In Esau's case, these privileges were the greater, for
they were the direct gift of God. Esau, as being the eldest born of his

father Isaac, inherited certain rights and privileges that Isaac, the long-expected heir of Abraham, had received from Abraham. Now Esau's sin, when he was a young man, had been this — he parted with his birthright to his younger brother Jacob. He thought lightly of God's great gift. How little he thought of it is plain by the price he took for it. Esau had been hunting, and he came home tired and faint. Jacob, who had remained at home, had some pottage; and Esau begged for some of it. Jacob knew the worth of the birthright, though Esau did not; he had faith to discern it. So when Esau asked for pottage, he said he would give it to Esau in exchange for his birthright; and Esau, caring nothing for the birthright, sold it to Jacob for the mess of food. This was a great sin, as being a contempt of a special gift of God, a gift that, after his father, Isaac, no one in the whole world had but he.

Time went on. Esau got older and understood more than before the value of the gift that he had thus profanely surrendered. Doubtless he would fain have got it back again if he could; but that was impossible. Under these circumstances, as we find in the chapter that has been read in the course of today's Service, his father proposed to give him his solemn blessing before he died. Now this blessing in those times carried great weight with it, as being of the nature of a prophecy, and it had been from the first divinely intended for Jacob; Esau had no right to it, but he thought that in this way he should in a certain sense get back his birthright, or what would stand in its place. He had parted with it easily, and he expected to regain it easily. Observe, he showed no repentance for what he had done, no self-reproach; he had no fear that God would punish him. He only regretted his loss, without humbling himself; and he determined to retrace his steps as quickly and quietly as he could. He went to hunt for venison and dress it as savory meat for his father, as his father bade him. And having got all ready, he came with it and stood before his father. Then was it that he learned, to his misery, that God's gifts are not thus lightly to be treated; he had sold, he could not recover. He had hoped to have had his father's blessing, but Jacob had received it instead. He had thought to regain God's favor not by fasting and prayer but by savory meat, by feasting and making merry.

Such seems, on the whole, St. Paul's account of the matter in his Epistle to the Hebrews. After having given examples of faith, he bids his Christian brethren beware lest there should be anyone among them like Esau, whom he calls a "profane person," as having thought and acted with so little of real perception of things unseen; "looking diligently," he says, "lest any man fail of the grace of God … lest there be any fornicator, or profane person, as Esau, who for one morsel of meat sold his birthright. For ye know how that afterward, when he would have inherited the blessing, he was rejected; for he found no place of repentance, though he sought it carefully with tears" (Heb. 12:15–17).

This, then, is the meaning of Esau's great and bitter cry, which at first sight we are disposed to pity. It is the cry of one who has rejected God, and God in turn has rejected him. It is the cry of one who has trifled with God's mercies and then sought to regain them when it was all too late. It is the cry of one who has not heeded the warning, "See that ye receive not the grace of God in vain" and who has "come short of the glory of God" (2 Cor. 6:1; Rom. 3:23). It is the cry predicted by the wise man, "Then shall they call upon Me, but I will not answer; they shall seek Me early, but they shall not find Me" (Prov. 1:28). That subtilty and keenness of his brother Jacob, by which he got before him and took the Kingdom of Heaven by violence, was God's act; it was God's providence punishing Esau for former sin. Esau had sinned; he had forfeited his birthright, and he could not get it back. That cry of his, what was it like? It was like the entreaty of the five foolish virgins when the door was shut, "Lord, Lord, open to us; but He answered and said, Verily, I say unto you, I know you not"

(Matt. 25:11–12). It was like the "weeping and gnashing of teeth" of lost souls (Matt. 25:30). Yes, surely, a great and bitter cry it well might be. Well may they weep and cry, as they will most largely, who have received God's grace and done despite to it.

The mournful history, then, that I have been reviewing is a description of one who was first profane and then presumptuous. Esau was profane in selling his birthright, he was presumptuous in claiming the blessing. Afterward, indeed, he did repent, but when it was too late. And I fear such as Esau was of old time, such are too many Christians now. They despise God's blessings when they are young and strong and healthy; then, when they get old or weak or sick, they do not think of repenting, but they think they may take and enjoy the privileges of the gospel as a matter of course, as if the sins of former years went for nothing. And then, perhaps, death comes upon them; and then after death, when it is too late, they would fain repent. Then they utter a great, bitter, and piercing cry to God; and when they see happy souls ascending toward Heaven in the fullness of Gospel blessings, they say to their offended God, "Bless me, even me also, O my Father."

Is it not, I say, quite a common case for men and for women to neglect religion in their best days? They have been baptized, they have been taught their duty, they have been taught to pray, they know their Creed, their conscience has been enlightened, they have opportunity to come to Church. This is their birthright, the privileges of their birth of water and of the Spirit; but they sell it, as Esau did. They are tempted by Satan with some bribe of this world, and they give up their birthright in exchange for what is sure to perish, and to make them perish with it. Esau was tempted by the mess of pottage that he saw in Jacob's hands. Satan arrested the eyes of his lust, and he gazed on the pottage as Eve gazed on the fruit of the tree of knowledge of good and evil. Adam and Eve sold their birthright for the fruit of a tree — that was their bargain. Esau sold his for a mess of lentils — that was his. And men nowadays often sell theirs not indeed for anything so simple as fruit or herbs, but for some evil gain or other that at the time they think worth purchasing at any price; perhaps for the enjoyment of some particular sin, or more commonly for the indulgence of general carelessness and spiritual sloth, because they do not like a strict life and have no heart for God's service. And thus they are profane persons, for they despise the great gift of God.

And then, when all is done and over, and their souls sold to Satan, they never seem to understand that they have *parted* with their birthright. They think that they stand just where they did before they followed the world, the flesh, and the devil; they take for granted that when they choose to become more decent, or more religious, they have all their privileges just as before. Like Samson, they propose to go out as at other times before and shake themselves. And like Esau, instead of repenting for the loss of the birthright, they come, as a matter of course, for the blessing. Esau went out to hunt for venison gaily and promptly brought it to his father. His spirits were high, his voice was cheerful. It did not strike him that God was angry with him for what had passed years ago. He thought he was as sure of the blessing as if he had *not* sold the birthright.

And then, alas! The truth flashed upon him; he uttered a great and bitter cry when it was too late. It would have been well had he uttered it before he came for the blessing, not after it. He repented when it was too late — it had been well if he had repented in time. So I say of persons who have in any way sinned. It is good for them not to forget that they have sinned. It is good that they should lament and deplore their past sins. Depend upon it, they will wail over them in the next world, if they wail not here. Which is better, to utter a bitter cry now or then? Then, when the blessing of eternal life is refused them by the just Judge at the Last Day, or now, in order that they may gain it? Let us be wise enough to have our agony in this world, not in the next. If we humble ourselves now, God will pardon us then. We cannot escape punishment, here or hereafter; we must take our choice, whether to suffer and mourn a little now, or much then.

Would you see how a penitent should come to God? Turn to the parable of the Prodigal Son. He, too, had squandered away his birthright, as Esau did. He, too, came for the blessing, like Esau. Yes; but how differently he came! He came with deep confession and self-abasement. He said, "Father, I have sinned against Heaven and before thee, and am no more worthy to be called thy son: make me as one of thy hired servants (see Luke 15:21); but Esau said, "Let my father arise, and eat of his son's venison, that thy soul may bless me" (Gen. 27:31). The one came for a son's privileges, the other for a servant's drudgery. The one killed and dressed his venison with his own hand and enjoyed it not; for the other the fatted calf was prepared, and the ring for his hand, and shoes for his feet, and the best robe, and there was music and dancing.

These are thoughts, I need hardly say, especially suited to this season. From the earliest times down to this day, these weeks before Easter have been set apart every year for the particular remembrance and confession of our sins. From the first age downward, not a year has passed but Christians have been exhorted to reflect how far they have let go their birthright, as a preparation for their claiming the blessing. At Christmas we are born again with Christ; at Easter we keep the Eucharistic Feast. In Lent, by penance, we join the two great sacraments together. Are you, my brethren, prepared to say — is there any single Christian alive who will dare to profess — that he has not in greater or less degree sinned against God's free mercies as bestowed on him in Baptism without, or rather against, his deserts? Who will say that he has so improved his birthright that the blessing is his fit reward without either sin to confess or wrath to deprecate? See, then, the Church offers you this season for the purpose. "Now is the accepted time, now the day of salvation" (2 Cor. 6:2). Now it is that, God being your helper, you are to attempt to throw off from you the heavy burden of past transgression, to reconcile yourselves to Him who has once already imparted to you His atoning merits, and you have profaned them.

And be sure of this: that if He has any love for you, if He sees aught of good in your soul, *He* will afflict you, if you will not afflict yourselves. He will not let you escape. He has ten thousand ways of purging those whom He has chosen from the dross and alloy with which the fine gold is defaced. He can bring diseases on you, or can visit you with misfortunes, or take away your friends, or oppress your minds with darkness, or refuse you strength to bear up against pain when it comes upon you. He can inflict on you a lingering and painful death. He can make "the bitterness of death" pass not (1 Sam. 15:32). We, indeed, cannot decide in the case of others when trouble is a punishment and when not; yet this we know, that all sin brings affliction. We have no means of judging others, but we may judge ourselves. Let us judge ourselves that we be not judged. Let us afflict ourselves that God may not afflict us. Let us come before Him with our best offerings so that He may forgive us.

Such advice is especially suitable to an age like this, when there is an effort on all hands to multiply comforts and to get rid of the daily inconveniences and distresses of life. Alas! My brethren, how do you know, if you avail yourselves of the luxuries of this world without restraint, but that you are only postponing, and increasing by postponing, an inevitable chastisement? How do you know but that if you will not satisfy the debt of daily sin now, it will hereafter come upon you with interest? See whether this is not a thought that would spoil that enjoyment that even religious persons are apt to take in this world's goods, if they would but admit it. It is said that we ought to enjoy this life as the gift of God. Easy circumstances are generally thought a special happiness; it is thought a great point to get rid of annoyance or discomfort of mind and body; it is thought allowable and suitable to make use of all means available for making life pleasant. We desire, and confess we desire, to make time pass agreeably and to live in the sunshine. All things harsh and austere are carefully put aside. We shrink from the rude lap of earth, and the embrace of the elements, and we build ourselves houses in which the flesh may enjoy its lust and the eye its pride. We aim at having all things at our will. Cold, and hunger, and hard lodging, and ill usage, and humble offices, and mean appearance, are all considered serious evils. And thus year follows year, tomorrow as today, till we think that this, our artificial life, is our natural state, and must and ever will be. But, O ye sons and daughters of men, what if this fair weather but ensure the storm afterward? What if it be that the nearer you attain to making yourselves as gods on earth now, the greater pain lies before you in time to come, or even (if it must be said) the more certain becomes your ruin when time is at an end? Come down, then, from your high chambers at this season to avert what else may be. Sinners as ye are, act at least like the prosperous heathen who threw his choicest trinket into the water that he might propitiate fortune. Let not the year go round and round without a break and interruption in its circle of pleasures. Give back some of God's gifts to God that you may safely enjoy the rest. Fast, or watch, or abound in alms, or be instant in prayer, or deny yourselves society, or pleasant books, or easy clothing, or take on you some irksome task or employment; do one or other, or some, or all of these, unless you say that you have never sinned and may go like Esau with a light heart to take your crown. Ever bear in mind that day that will reveal all things and will test all things "so as by fire" (1 Cor. 3:15), and that will bring us into judgment ere it lodges us in Heaven.

And for those who have in any grievous way sinned or neglected God, I recommend such persons never to forget they *have* sinned; if they forget it not, God in mercy *will* forget it. I recommend them every day, morning and evening, to fall on their knees and say, "Lord, forgive me my past sins." I recommend them to pray God to visit their sins in this world rather than in the next. I recommend them to go over their dreadful sins in their minds (unless, alas, it makes them sin afresh to do so), and to confess them to God again and again with great shame, and to entreat His pardon. I recommend them to look on all pain and sorrow that comes on them as a *punishment* for what they once were, and to take it patiently on that account, nay, joyfully, as giving them a hope that God is punishing them here instead of hereafter. If they have committed sins of uncleanness and are now in narrow circumstances or have undutiful children, let them take their present distress as God's merciful punishment. If they have lived to the world and now have worldly anxieties, these anxieties are God's punishment. If they have led intemperate lives and now are afflicted by any malady, this is God's punishment. Let them not cease to pray, under all circumstances, that God will pardon them and give them back what they have lost. And thus, by God's grace, it shall be restored to them, and Esau's great and bitter cry never shall be theirs.

CHAPTER 6

The Humiliation of the Eternal Son

*"Who, in the days of His flesh, when He had offered up
prayers and supplications with strong crying and tears
unto Him that was able to save Him from death, and
was heard in that He feared, though He were a Son, yet
learned He obedience by the things which He suffered."*

Hebrews 5:7–8

THE CHIEF MYSTERY OF our holy faith is the humiliation of the
Son of God to temptation and suffering, as described in this passage
of Scripture. In truth, it is a more overwhelming mystery even than
that which is involved in the doctrine of the Trinity. I say more
overwhelming, not greater — for we cannot measure the more and
the less in subjects utterly incomprehensible and divine — but with
more in it to perplex and subdue our minds. When the mystery of
the Trinity is set before us, we see indeed that it is quite beyond our
reason; but, at the same time, it is no wonder that human language
should be unable to convey, and human intellect to receive, truths
relating to the incommunicable and infinite essence of Almighty
God. But the mystery of the Incarnation relates, in part, to subjects
more level with our reason; it lies not only in the manner how God
and man is one Christ, but in the very fact that so it is. We think we

know of God so much as this, that He is altogether separate from imperfection and infirmity; yet we are told that the Eternal Son has taken into Himself a creature's nature that henceforth became as much one with Him, as much belonged to Him, as the divine attributes and powers that He had ever had. The mystery lies as much in what we think we know as in what we do not know. Reflect, for instance, upon the language of the text. The Son of God, who had glory with the Father from everlasting (see John 17:5), was found, at a certain time, in human flesh, offering up prayers and supplications to Him, crying out and weeping, and exercising obedience in suffering! Do not suppose, from my thus speaking, that I would put the doctrine before you as a hard saying, as a stumbling block and a yoke of bondage to which you must perforce submit, however unwillingly. Far be it from us to take such unthankful account of a dispensation that has brought us salvation! Those who in the Cross of Christ see the Atonement for sin cannot choose but glory in it; and its mysteriousness does but make them glory in it the more. They boast of it before men and angels, before an unbelieving world, and before fallen spirits; with no confusion of face but with a reverent boldness, they confess this miracle of grace and cherish it in their creed, though it gains them but the contempt and derision of the proud and ungodly.

And as the doctrine of our Lord's humiliation is most mysterious, so the very surface of the narrative in which it is contained is mysterious also as exciting wonder and impressing upon us our real ignorance of the nature, manner, and causes of it. Take, for instance, His temptation. Why was it undergone at all, seeing our redemption is ascribed to His death, not to it? Why was it so long? What took place during it? What was Satan's particular object in tempting Him? How came Satan to have such power over Him as to be able to transport Him from place to place? And what was the precise result of the temptation? These and many other questions admit of no satisfactory solution. There is something remarkable, too, in the period of it, being the same as that of the long fasts of Moses and Elijah and of His own abode on earth after His Resurrection. A like mystery again is cast around that last period of His earthly mission. Then He was engaged we know not how, except that He appeared, from time to time, to His apostles; of the forty days of His temptation we know still less, only that "He did eat nothing" and "was with the wild beasts" (Luke 4:2; Mark 1:13).

Again, there is something of mystery in the connection of His temptation with the descent of the Holy Ghost upon Him on His Baptism. After the voice from Heaven had proclaimed, "Thou art My beloved Son, in whom I am well pleased," "*immediately,*" as St. Mark says, "the Spirit *driveth* Him into the wilderness" (Mark 1:11–12). As if there were some connection, beyond our understanding, between His Baptism and temptation, the first act of the Holy Spirit is forthwith to "drive Him" (whatever is meant by the word) into the wilderness. Observe, too, that it was almost from this solemn recognition, "Thou art My beloved Son," that the devil took up the temptation, "*If* Thou be the Son of God, command that these stones be made bread" (Matt. 4:3), yet what his thoughts and designs were, we cannot even conjecture. All we see is a renewal, apparently, of Adam's temptation, in the person of the "second Man" (1 Cor. 15:47).

In like manner, questions might be asked concerning His descent into Hell, which could as little be solved with our present limited knowledge of the nature and means of His gracious economy.

I bring together these various questions in order to impress upon you our depth of ignorance on the entire subject under review. The dispensation of mercy is revealed to us in its great and blessed result, our redemption, and in one or two other momentous points. Upon all these we ought to dwell and enlarge, mindfully and thankfully, but with the constant recollection that after all, as regards the dispensation itself, only one or two partial notices are revealed to us altogether of a great divine work. Enlarge upon them we ought, even because they are few and partial, not slighting what is given us, because it is not all (like the servant who buried his lord's talent), but giving it what increase we can. And as there is much danger of the narrow spirit of that slothful servant at the present day, in which is strangely combined a profession of knowing everything with an assertion that there is nothing to know concerning the Incarnation, I propose now, by God's blessing, to set before you the Scripture doctrine concerning it as the Church Catholic has ever received it, trading with the talent committed to us so that when our Lord comes He may receive His own with usury.

Bearing in mind, then, that we know nothing truly about the manner or the ultimate ends of the humiliation of the Eternal Son, our Lord and Savior, let us consider what that humiliation itself was.

The text says, "though He were a Son" (Heb. 5:8). Now, in these words, "the Son of God," much more is implied than at first sight may appear. Many a man gathers up, here and there, some fragments of religious knowledge. He hears one thing said in Church, he sees another thing in the prayerbook, and among religious people, or in the world, he gains something more. In this way, he gets possession of sacred words and statements, knowing very little about them really. He interprets them, as it may happen, according to the various and inconsistent opinions that he has met with, or he puts his own meaning upon them, that is, the meaning, as must needs be, of an untaught, not to say a carnal and irreverent, mind. How can a man expect he shall discern and apprehend the real meaning and language of Scripture if he has never approached it as a learner and waited on the Divine Author of it for the gift of wisdom? By continual meditation on the sacred text, by diligent use of the Church's instruction, he will come to understand what the Gospel doctrines are; but most surely, if all the knowledge he has be gathered from a sentence caught up here and an argument heard there, even when he is most orthodox in word, he has but a collection of phrases, on which he puts not the right meaning but his own meaning. And the least reflection must show you what a very poor and unworthy meaning, or rather how false a meaning, "the natural man" will put upon "the things of the Spirit of God" (1 Cor. 2:14). I have been led to say this from having used the words "the Son of God," which, I much fear, convey, to a great many minds, little or no idea, little or nothing of a high, religious, solemn idea. We have, perhaps, a vague general notion that they mean something extraordinary and supernatural; but we know that we ourselves are called, in one sense, sons of God in Scripture.[3] Moreover, we have heard, perhaps (and even though we do not recollect it, yet may retain the impression of it), that the angels are sons of God. In consequence, we collect just thus much from the title as applied to our Lord, that He came from God, that He was the well-beloved of God, and that He is much more than a mere man. This is all that the words convey to many men at the most, while many more refer them merely to His human nature. How different is the state of those who have been duly initiated into the mysteries of the Kingdom of Heaven! How different was the mind of the primitive Christians, who so eagerly and vigorously apprehended the gracious announcement that in this title, "the Son of God," they saw and enjoyed the full glories of the gospel doctrine! When times grew cold and unbelieving, then indeed, as at this day, public

---

[3]   See John 1:12; Rom. 8:14; 1 John 3:1–2.

explanations were necessary of those simple and sacred words; but the first Christians needed none. They felt that in saying that Christ was the Son of God, they were witnessing to a thousand marvelous and salutary truths that they could not indeed understand but by which they might gain life and for which they could dare to die.

What, then, is meant by the "Son of God"? It is meant that our Lord is the very or true Son of God, that is, His Son by nature. We are but *called* the sons of God — we are adopted to be sons — but our Lord and Savior is the Son of God, really and by birth, and He alone is such. Hence Scripture calls Him the only begotten Son (John 3:16). "Such knowledge is too excellent for" us (Ps. 139:6); yet however high it be, we learn as from His own mouth that God is not solitary, if we may dare so to speak, but that in His own incomprehensible essence, in His perfection of His one indivisible and eternal nature, His dearly beloved Son has ever existed with Him, who is called the Word and, being His Son, is partaker in all the fullness of His Godhead. "In the beginning was the Word, and the Word was with God, and the Word was God" (John 1:1). Thus when the early Christians used the title "the Son of God," they meant, after the manner of the apostles when they use it in Scripture, all we mean in the Creed when, by way of explaining ourselves, we confess Him to be "God from God, Light from Light, True God from True God." For in that He is the Son of God, He must be whatever God is, all-holy, all-wise, all-powerful, all-good, eternal, infinite; yet since there is only one God, He must be at the same time not separate from God, but ever one with and in Him, one indivisibly; so that it would be as idle language to speak of Him as separated in essence from His Father as to say that our reason, or intellect, or will, was separate from our minds; as rash and profane language to deny to the Father His Only-begotten Word, in whom He has ever delighted, as to deny His

Wisdom or Goodness, or Power, which also have been in and with Him from everlasting.

The text goes on to say, "Though He were a Son, yet learned He obedience by the things which He suffered." Obedience belongs to a servant, but accordance, concurrence, cooperation, are the characteristics of a Son. In His eternal union with God, there was no distinction of will and work between Him and His Father; as the Father's life was the Son's life, and the Father's glory the Son's also, so the Son was the very Word and Wisdom of the Father, His Power and Coequal Minister in all things, the same and not the same as He Himself. But in the days of His flesh, when He had humbled Himself to "the form of a servant" (Phil. 2:7), taking on Himself a separate will and a separate work, and the toil and sufferings incident to a creature, then what had been mere concurrence became obedience. This, then, is the force of the words,

"Though He was a Son, yet had He experience of *obedience*." He took on Him a lower nature and wrought in it toward a Will higher and more perfect than it. Further, "He learned obedience amid *suffering*," and, therefore, amid temptation. His mysterious agony under it is described in the former part of the text, which declares that "in the days of His flesh," He "offered up prayers and supplications, with strong crying and tears, unto Him that was able to save Him from death, and was heard in that He feared" (Heb. 5:7). Or, in the words of the foregoing chapter, He "was in all points tempted like as we are, yet without sin" (Heb. 4:15).

I am only concerned here in setting before you the sacred truth itself, not how it was, or why, or with what result. Let us, then, reverently consider what is implied in it. "The Word was made flesh" (John 1:14); by which is meant not that He selected some particular existing man and dwelt in him (which in no sense would answer to the force of those words, and which He condescends to do continually in the case of all His elect, through His Spirit), but that He became what He was not before, that He took into His own Infinite Essence man's nature itself in all its completeness, creating a soul and body and, at the moment of creation, making them His own, so that they never were other than His, never existed by themselves or except as in Him, being properties or attributes of Him (to use defective words) as really as His divine goodness, or His eternal Sonship, or His perfect likeness to the Father. And while thus adding a new nature to Himself, He did not in any respect cease to be what He was before. How was that possible? All the while He was on earth, when He was conceived, when He was born, when He was tempted, on the Cross, in the grave, and now at God's right hand — all the time through, He was the Eternal and Unchangeable Word, the Son of God. The flesh that He had assumed was but the instrument through which He acted for and toward us. As He acts in creation by His wisdom and power, toward angels by His love, toward devils by His wrath, so He has acted for our redemption through our own nature, which in His great mercy He attached to His own Person, as if an attribute, simply, absolutely, indissolubly. Thus St. Paul speaks — as in other places, of the love of God and the holiness of God — so in one place expressly of "the blood of God," if I may venture to use such words out of the sacred context. "Feed the Church of God," he says to the elders of Ephesus, "which He hath purchased with *His own blood*" (Acts 20:28). Accordingly, whatever our Lord said or did upon earth was strictly and literally the word and deed of God Himself. Just as we speak of seeing our friends, though we do not see their souls but merely their bodies, so the apostles, disciples, priests, Pharisees, and the multitude, all who saw Christ in the flesh, saw, as the whole earth will see at the Last Day, the Very and Eternal Son of God.

After this manner, then, must be understood His suffering, temptation, and obedience, not as if He ceased to be what He had ever been, but, having clothed Himself with a created essence, He made it the instrument of His humiliation; He acted in it, He obeyed and suffered through it. Do not we see among men circumstances of a peculiar kind throw one of our own race out of himself, so that he, the same man, acts as if his usual self were not in being and he had fresh feelings and faculties, for the occasion, higher or lower than before? Far be it from our thoughts to parallel the Incarnation of the Eternal Word with such an accidental change! But I mention it not to explain a Mystery (which I relinquished the thought of from the first) but to facilitate your *conception* of Him who is the subject of it, to help you toward contemplating Him as God and man at once, as still the Son of God though He had assumed a nature short of His original perfection. That Eternal Power, which, till then, had thought and acted as God, began to think and act as a man, with all man's faculties, affections, and imperfections, sin excepted. Before He came on earth, He was infinitely above joy and grief, fear and anger, pain and heaviness; but afterward, all these properties and many more were His as fully as they are ours. Before He came on earth, He had but the perfections of God, but afterward He had also the virtues of a creature, such as faith, meekness, self-denial. Before He came on earth, He could not be tempted of evil; but afterward He had a man's heart, a man's tears, and a man's wants and infirmities. His divine nature indeed pervaded His manhood, so that every deed and word of His in the flesh savored of eternity and infinity; but, on the other hand, from the time He was born of the Virgin Mary, he had a natural fear of danger, a natural shrinking from pain, though ever subject to the ruling influence of that Holy and Eternal Essence that was in Him. For instance, we read on one occasion of His praying that the cup might pass from Him; and at another, when Peter showed surprise at the prospect of His Crucifixion, He rebuked him sharply, as if for tempting Him to murmur and disobey.

Thus He possessed at once a double assemblage of attributes, divine and human. Still he was all-powerful, though in the form of a servant; still He was all-knowing, though seemingly ignorant; still incapable of temptation, though exposed to it; and if anyone stumble at this, as not a mere mystery but in the very form of language a contradiction of terms, I would have him reflect on those peculiarities of human nature itself, which I just now hinted at. Let him consider the condition of his own mind and see how like a contradiction it is. Let him reflect upon the faculty of memory and try to determine whether he does or does not know a thing that he cannot recollect, or rather, whether it may not be said of him, that one self-same person, that in one sense he knows it, in another he does not know it. This may serve to appease his imagination if it startles at the mystery. Or let him consider the state of an infant, who seems, indeed, to be without a soul for many months, who seems to have only the senses and functions of animal life, yet has, we know, a soul, which may even be regenerated. What, indeed, can be more mysterious than the Baptism of an infant? How strange is it, yet how transporting a sight, what a source of meditation is opened on us, while we look upon what seems so helpless, so reasonless, and know that at that moment it has a soul so fully formed, as on the one hand, indeed, to be a child of wrath, and on the other (blessed be God), to be capable of a new birth through the Spirit! Who can say, if we had eyes to see, in what state that infant soul is? Who can say it has not its energies of reason and of will in some unknown sphere, quite consistently with the reality of its insensibility to the external world? Who can say that all of us, or at least all who are living in the faith of Christ, have not some strange but

unconscious life in God's presence all the while we are here, seeing
what we do not know we see, impressed yet without power of reflection, and this, without having a double self in consequence, and
with an increase to us, not a diminution, of the practical reality of
our earthly sojourn and probation? Are there not men before now
who, like Elisha when his spirit followed Gehazi, or St. Peter when
he announced the coming of Sapphira's bearers, or St. Paul when
his presence went before him to Corinth (2 Kings 5:26; Acts 5:9; 1
Cor. 4:19; 5:3), seem to range beyond themselves, even while in
the flesh? Who knows where he is "in visions of the night" (Job
33:15)? And this being so, how can we pronounce it to be any contradiction that while the Word of God was upon earth, in our flesh,
compassed within and without with human virtues and feelings,
with faith and patience, fear and joy, grief, misgivings, infirmities,
temptations, still He was, according to His divine nature, as from
the first, passing in thought from one end of Heaven even to the
other, reading all hearts, foreseeing all events, and receiving all worship as in the bosom of the Father? This, indeed, is what He
suggests to us Himself in those surprising words addressed to Nicodemus, which might even be taken to imply that even His human
nature was at that very time in Heaven while He spoke to him. "No
man hath ascended up to Heaven, but He that came down from
Heaven, even the Son of man which is in Heaven" (John 3:13).

To conclude, if anyone is tempted to consider such subjects as
the foregoing abstract, speculative, and unprofitable, I would observe, in answer, that I have taken it on the very ground of its being,
as I believe, especially practical. Let it not be thought a strange
thing to say, though I say it, that there is much in the religious belief, even of the more serious part of the community at present, to
make observant men very anxious where it will end. It would be no
very difficult matter, I suspect, to perplex the faith of a great many

persons who believe themselves to be orthodox and, indeed, are so, according to their light. They have been accustomed to call Christ God, but that is all; they have not considered what is meant by applying that title to One who was really a man, and from the vague way in which they use it, they would be in no small danger, if assailed by a subtle disputant, of being robbed of the sacred truth in its substance, even if they kept it in name. In truth, until we contemplate our Lord and Savior, God and man, as a really existing being, external to our minds, as complete and entire in His personality as we show ourselves to be to each other, as one and the same in all His various and contrary attributes, "the same yesterday, today, and forever" (Heb. 13:8), we are using words that profit not. Till then we do not realize that object of faith that is not a mere name on which titles and properties may be affixed without congruity and meaning but has a personal existence and an identity distinct from everything else. In what true sense do we "know" Him if our idea of Him be not such as to take up and incorporate into itself the manifold attributes and offices that we ascribe to Him? What do we gain from words, however correct and abundant, if they end with themselves, instead of lighting up the image of the Incarnate Son in our hearts? Yet this charge may too surely be brought against the theology of late centuries that, under the pretense of guarding against presumption, denies us what is revealed, like Ahaz refusing to ask for a sign lest it should tempt the Lord (Isa. 7:10–12).

Influenced by it, we have well-nigh forgotten the sacred truth, graciously disclosed for our support, that Christ is the Son of God in His divine nature as well as His human; we have well-nigh ceased to regard Him, after the pattern of the Nicene Creed, as "God from God, Light from Light," ever one with Him, yet ever distinct from Him. We speak of Him in a vague way as God, which is true, but not the whole truth; and in consequence, when we proceed to consider His humiliation, we are unable to carry on the notion of His personality from Heaven to earth. He who was but now spoken of as God, without mention of the Father from whom He is, is next described as if a creature; but how do these distinct notions of Him hold together in our minds? We are able indeed to continue the idea of a Son into that of a servant, though the descent was infinite and, to our reason, incomprehensible; but when we merely speak first of God, then of man, we seem to change the Nature without preserving the Person. In truth, His divine Sonship is that portion of the sacred doctrine on which the mind is providentially intended to rest throughout and so to preserve for itself His identity unbroken. But when we abandon this gracious help afforded to our faith, how can we hope to gain the one true and simple vision of Him? How shall we possibly look beyond our own words or apprehend, in any sort, what we say? In consequence, we are too often led, as a matter of necessity, in discoursing of His words and works, to distinguish between the Christ who lived on earth and the Son of God Most High, speaking of His human nature and His divine nature so separately as not to feel or understand that God is man and man is God. I am speaking of those of us who have learned to reflect, reason, and dispute, to inquire and pursue their thoughts, not of the incurious or illiterate who are not exposed to the temptation in question; and of the former I fear I must say (to use the language of ancient theology) that they begin by being Sabellians, that they go on to be Nestorians, and that they tend to be Ebionites and to deny Christ's divinity altogether. Meanwhile, the religious world little thinks whither its opinions are leading, and it will not discover that it is adoring a mere abstract name or a vague creation of the mind for the ever-living Son till the defection of its members from the Faith startle it and teach it that the so-called religion of the heart, without orthodoxy of doctrine, is but the warmth of a corpse: real for a time, but sure to fail.

How long will that complicated error last under which our Church now labors? How long are human traditions of modern date to obscure, in so many ways, the majestic interpretations of Holy Writ that the Church Catholic has inherited from the age of the apostles? When shall we be content to enjoy the wisdom and the pureness that Christ has bequeathed to His Church as a perpetual gift, instead of attempting to draw our Creed, each for himself, as he best may, from the deep wells of truth? Surely in vain have we escaped from the superstitions of the Middle Ages if the corruptions of a rash and self-trusting philosophy spread over our faith!

May God, even the Father, give us a heart and understanding to realize as well as to confess that doctrine into which we were baptized, that His Only-begotten Son, our Lord, was conceived by the Holy Ghost, was born of the Virgin Mary, suffered, and was buried, rose again from the dead, ascended into Heaven, from whence He shall come again, at the end of the world, to judge the quick and the dead.

CHAPTER 7

The Cross of Christ:
The Measure of the World

"And I, if I be lifted up from the earth,
will draw all men unto Me."

John 12:32

SIXTH SUNDAY IN LENT

A GREAT NUMBER OF men live and die without reflecting at all
upon the state of things in which they find themselves. They take
things as they come and follow their inclinations as far as they have
the opportunity. They are guided mainly by pleasure and pain, not
by reason, principle, or conscience; and they do not attempt to
interpret this world, to determine what it means, or to reduce what
they see and feel to system. But when persons, either from thought-
fulness of mind or from intellectual activity, begin to contemplate
the visible state of things into which they are born, then forthwith
they find it a maze and a perplexity. It is a riddle that they cannot
solve. It seems full of contradictions and without a drift. Why it
is, and what it is to issue in, and how it is what it is, and how we
come to be introduced into it, and what is our destiny, are all
mysteries.

In this difficulty, some have formed one philosophy of life, and others another. Men have thought they had found the key by means of which they might read what is so obscure. Ten thousand things come before us one after another in the course of life, and what are we to think of them? What color are we to give them? Are we to look at all things in a gay and mirthful way? Or in a melancholy way? In a desponding or a hopeful way? Are we to make light of life altogether, or to treat the whole subject seriously? Are we to make greatest things of little consequence, or least things of great consequence? Are we to keep in mind what is past and gone, or are we to look on to the future, or are we to be absorbed in what is present? How are we to look at things? This is the question that all persons of observation ask themselves, and answer each in his own way. They wish to think by rule, by something within them that may harmonize and adjust what is without them. Such is the need felt by reflective minds. Now, let me ask, what is the real key, what is the Christian interpretation of this world? What is given us by revelation to estimate and measure this world by? The event of this season — the Crucifixion of the Son of God.

It is the death of the Eternal Word of God made flesh that is our great lesson how to think and how to speak of this world. His Cross has put its due value upon everything that we see, upon all fortunes, all advantages, all ranks, all dignities, all pleasures; upon the lust of the flesh, and the lust of the eyes, and the pride of life. It has set a price upon the excitements, the rivalries, the hopes, the fears, the desires, the efforts, the triumphs of mortal man. It has given a meaning to the various, shifting course, the trials, the temptations, the sufferings, of his earthly state. It has brought together and made consistent all that seemed discordant and aimless. It has taught us how to live, how to use this world, what to expect, what to desire, what to hope. It is the tone into which all the strains of this world's music are ultimately to be resolved.

Look around and see what the world presents of high and low. Go to the court of princes. See the treasure and skill of all nations brought together to honor a child of man. Observe the prostration of the many before the few. Consider the form and ceremonial, the pomp, the state, the circumstance — and the vainglory. Do you wish to know the worth of it all? Look at the Cross of Christ.

Go to the political world: see nation jealous of nation, trade rivaling trade, armies and fleets matched against each other. Survey the various ranks of the community, its parties and their contests, the strivings of the ambitious, the intrigues of the crafty. What is the end of all this turmoil? The grave. What is the measure? The Cross.

Go, again, to the world of intellect and science: consider the wonderful discoveries that the human mind is making, the variety of arts to which its discoveries give rise, the all but miracles by which it shows its power; and next, the pride and confidence of reason and the absorbing devotion of thought to transitory objects, which is the consequence. Would you form a right judgment of all this? Look at the Cross.

Again: look at misery, look at poverty and destitution, look at oppression and captivity; go where food is scanty and lodging unhealthy. Consider pain and suffering, diseases long or violent, all that is frightful and revolting. Would you know how to rate all these? Gaze upon the Cross.

Thus in the Cross, and Him who hung upon it, all things meet; all things subserve it, all things need it. It is their center and their interpretation. For He was lifted up upon it that He might draw all men and all things unto Him.

But it will be said that the view that the Cross of Christ imparts to us of human life and of the world is not that which we should take, if left to ourselves; that it is not an obvious view; that if we look at things on their surface, they are far more bright and sunny than they appear when viewed in the light that this season casts upon them. The world seems made for the enjoyment of just such a being as man, and man is put into it. He has the capacity of enjoyment, and the world supplies the means. How natural this, what a simple as well as pleasant philosophy, yet how different from that of the Cross! The doctrine of the Cross, it may be said, disarranges two parts of a system that seem made for each other; it severs the fruit from the eater, the enjoyment from the enjoyer. How does this solve a problem? Does it not rather itself create one?

I answer, first, that whatever force this objection may have, surely it is merely a repetition of that which Eve felt and Satan urged in Eden; for did not the woman see that the forbidden tree was "good for food" and "a tree to be desired" (Gen. 3:6)? Well, then, is it wonderful that we, too, the descendants of the first pair, should still be in a world where there is a forbidden fruit, and that our trials should lie in being within reach of it, and our happiness in abstaining from it? The world, at first sight, appears made for pleasure, and the vision of Christ's Cross is a solemn and sorrowful sight interfering with this appearance. Be it so; but why may it not be our duty to abstain from enjoyment notwithstanding, if it was a duty even in Eden?

But again; it is but a superficial view of things to say that this life is made for pleasure and happiness. To those who look under the surface, it tells a very different tale. The doctrine of the Cross does but teach, though infinitely more forcibly, still after all it does but teach the very same lesson that this world teaches to those who live long in it, who have much experience in it, who know it. The world is sweet to the lips but bitter to the taste. It pleases at first but not at last. It looks gay on the outside, but evil and misery lie concealed within. When a man has passed a certain number of years in it, he cries out with the preacher, "Vanity of vanities, all is vanity" (Eccles. 1:2). Nay, if he has not religion for his guide, he will be forced to go further, and say, "All is vanity and vexation of spirit" (Eccles. 1:14); all is disappointment; all is sorrow; all is pain. The sore judgments of God upon sin are concealed within it, and they force a man to grieve whether he will or no. Therefore the doctrine of the Cross of Christ does but anticipate for us our experience of the world. It is true, it bids us grieve for our sins in the midst of all that smiles and glitters around us; but if we will not heed it, we shall at length be forced to grieve for them from undergoing their fearful punishment. If we will not acknowledge that this world has been made miserable by sin from the sight of Him on whom our sins were laid, we shall experience it to be miserable by the recoil of those sins upon ourselves.

It may be granted, then, that the doctrine of the Cross is not on the surface of the world. The surface of things is bright only, and the Cross is sorrowful; it is a hidden doctrine; it lies under a veil; it at first sight startles us, and we are tempted to revolt from it. Like St. Peter, we cry out, "Be it far from Thee, Lord; this shall not be unto Thee" (Matt. 16:22). And yet it is a true doctrine; for truth is not on the surface of things but in the depths.

And as the doctrine of the Cross, though it be the true interpretation of this world, is not prominently manifested in it upon its surface but is concealed, so again, when received into the faithful heart, there it abides as a living principle, but deep and hidden from observation. Religious men, in the words of Scripture, "live by the faith of the Son of God, who loved them and gave Himself for them" (Gal. 2:20), but they do not tell this to all men; they leave others to find it out as they may. Our Lord's own command to His disciples was that when they fast, they should "anoint their head and wash their face" (Matt. 6:17). Thus they are bound not to make a display but ever to be content to look outwardly different from what they are really inwardly. They are to carry a cheerful countenance with them and to control and regulate their feelings, that those feelings, by not being expended on the surface, may retire deep into their hearts and there live. And thus "Jesus Christ, and He crucified" is, as the apostle tells us, "a hidden wisdom" (1 Cor. 2:2, 7) — hidden in the world, which seems at first sight to speak a far other doctrine, and hidden in the faithful soul, which to persons at a distance, or to chance beholders, seems to be living but an ordinary life while really it is in secret holding communion with Him who was "manifest in the flesh," "crucified through weakness," "justified in the Spirit, seen of angels…, received up into glory" (1 Tim. 3:16; 2 Cor. 13:4).

This being the case, the great and awful doctrine of the Cross of Christ, which we now commemorate, may fitly be called, in the language of figure, the heart of religion. The heart may be considered as the seat of life; it is the principle of motion, heat, and activity; from it the blood goes to and fro to the extreme parts of the body.

It sustains the man in his powers and faculties; it enables the brain to think; and when it is touched, man dies. And in like manner, the sacred doctrine of Christ's Atoning Sacrifice is the vital principle on which the Christian lives and without which Christianity is not. Without it, no other doctrine is held profitably; to believe in Christ's divinity, or in His manhood, or in the Holy Trinity, or in a judgment to come, or in the resurrection of the dead, is an untrue belief, not Christian faith, unless we receive also the doctrine of Christ's sacrifice. On the other hand, to receive it presupposes the reception of other high truths of the gospel besides; it involves the belief in Christ's true divinity, in His true Incarnation, and in man's sinful state by nature; and it prepares the way to belief in the sacred Eucharistic feast, in which He who was once crucified is ever given to our souls and bodies, verily and indeed, in His Body and in His Blood. But again, the heart is hidden from view; it is carefully and securely guarded; it is not like the eye set in the forehead, commanding all, and seen of all: and so in like manner the sacred doctrine of the Atoning Sacrifice is not one to be talked of but to be lived upon; not to be put forth irreverently but to be adored secretly; not to be used as a necessary instrument in the conversion of the ungodly, or for the satisfaction of reasoners of this world, but to be unfolded to the docile and obedient: to young children, whom the world has not corrupted; to the sorrowful, who need comfort; to the sincere and earnest, who need a rule of life; to the innocent, who need warning; and to the established, who have earned the knowledge of it.

One more remark I shall make, and then conclude. It must not be supposed, because the doctrine of the Cross makes us sad, that therefore the gospel is a sad religion. The psalmist says, "They that sow in tears shall reap in joy;" and our Lord says, "They that mourn … shall be comforted" (Ps. 126:5; Matt. 5:4). Let no one go away with the impression that the gospel makes us take a gloomy view of the world and of life. It hinders us indeed from taking a superficial view and finding a vain transitory joy in what we see; but it forbids our immediate enjoyment only to grant enjoyment in truth and fullness afterward. It only forbids us to begin with enjoyment. It only says, if you begin with pleasure, you will end with pain. It bids us begin with the Cross of Christ, and in that Cross we shall at first find sorrow, but in a while peace and comfort will rise out of that sorrow. That Cross will lead us to mourning, repentance, humiliation, prayer, fasting; we shall sorrow for our sins, we shall sorrow with Christ's sufferings; but all this sorrow will only issue, nay, will be undergone in a happiness far greater than the enjoyment that the world gives — though careless, worldly minds indeed will not believe this, ridicule the notion of it, because they never have tasted it, and they will consider it a mere matter of words that religious persons think it decent and proper to use and try to believe themselves and to get others to believe, but that no one really feels. This is what they think; but our Savior said to His disciples, "Ye now therefore have sorrow, but I will see you again, and your heart shall rejoice, and your joy no man taketh from you," and "Peace I leave with you; My peace I give unto you; not as the world giveth, give I unto you" (John 16:22; 14:27). And St. Paul says, "The natural man receiveth not the things of the Spirit of God; for they are foolishness unto him; neither can he know them, because they are spiritually discerned," and "Eye hath not seen, nor ear heard, neither have entered into the heart of man, the things which God hath prepared for them that love Him" (1 Cor. 2:14, 9). And thus the Cross of Christ, as telling us of our redemption as well as of His sufferings, wounds us indeed, but so wounds as to heal also.

And thus, too, all that is bright and beautiful, even on the surface of this world, though it has no substance and may not suitably be enjoyed for its own sake, yet is a figure and promise of that true joy that issues out of the Atonement. It is a promise beforehand of what is to be: it is a shadow, raising hope because the substance is to follow, but not to be rashly taken instead of the substance. And it is God's usual mode of dealing with us in mercy to send the shadow before the substance, that we may take comfort in what is to be before it comes. Thus our Lord before His Passion rode into Jerusalem in triumph, with the multitudes crying Hosanna and strewing His road with palm branches and their garments. This was but a vain and hollow pageant, nor did our Lord take pleasure in it. It was a shadow that stayed not but flitted away. It could not be more than a shadow, for the Passion had not been undergone by which His true triumph was wrought out. He could not enter into His glory before He had first suffered. He could not take pleasure in this semblance of it, knowing that it was unreal. Yet that first shadowy triumph was the omen and presage of the true victory to come, when He had overcome the sharpness of death. And we commemorate this figurative triumph on the last Sunday in Lent to cheer us in the sorrow of the week that follows and to remind us of the true joy that comes with Easter Day.

And so, too, as regards this world, with all its enjoyments yet disappointments. Let us not trust it; let us not give our hearts to it; let us not begin with it. Let us begin with faith; let us begin with Christ; let us begin with His Cross and the humiliation to which it leads. Let us first be drawn to Him who is lifted up, that so He may, with Himself, freely give us all things. Let us "seek first the kingdom of God and His righteousness," and then all those things of this world will "be added to us" (Matt. 6:33). They alone are able truly to enjoy this world who begin with the world unseen. They alone enjoy it who have first abstained from it. They alone can truly feast who have first fasted; they alone are able to use the world who have learned not to abuse it; they alone inherit it who take it as a shadow of the world to come, and who for that world to come relinquish it.

Meditations on the Stations of the Cross

Mediations on the Stations of the Cross

Written about 1860;
used a second time, 1885. — J. H. N.

BEGIN WITH AN ACT OF CONTRITION

O MY GOD, I am heartily sorry for having offended Thee, and I detest all my sins because of Thy just punishments, but most of all because they offend Thee, my God, who are all good and deserving of all my love. I firmly resolve with the help of Thy grace to sin no more and to avoid the near occasion of sin. Amen.

Jesus Is Condemned to Death

℣. Adoramus te, Christe, et benedicimus tibi.

℟. Quia per sanctam Crucem tuam redemisti mundum.

℣. We adore Thee, O Christ, and we praise Thee.

℟. Because by Thy Holy Cross, Thou have redeemed the world.

Leaving the House of Caiphas, and dragged before Pilate and Herod, mocked, beaten, and spit upon, His back torn with scourges, His head crowned with thorns, Jesus, who on the Last Day will judge the world, is Himself condemned by unjust judges to a death of ignominy and torture.

Jesus is condemned to *death*. His death warrant is signed; and who signed it but I, when I committed my first mortal sins? My first mortal sins, when I fell away from the state of grace into which Thou didst place me by Baptism; these it was that were Thy death warrant, O Lord. The Innocent suffered for the guilty. Those sins of mine were the voices that cried out, "Let Him be crucified." That willingness and delight of heart with which I committed them was the consent that Pilate gave to this clamorous multitude. And the hardness of heart that followed upon them, my disgust, my despair, my proud impatience, my obstinate resolve to sin on, the love of sin that took possession of me — what were these contrary and impetuous feelings but the blows and the blasphemies with which the fierce soldiers and the populace received Thee, thus carrying out the sentence that Pilate had pronounced?

Pater, Ave, Gloria.	Our Father, Hail Mary, Glory Be.
℣. Miserere nostri, Domine.	℣. Have mercy on us, O Lord.
℟. Miserere nostri.	℟. Have mercy on us.
Fidelium animae, per misericordiam Dei, requiescant in pace. Amen.	May the souls of all the faithful departed, through the mercy of God, rest in peace. Amen.

THE SECOND STATION

Jesus Receives His Cross

℣. Adoramus te, Christe, et benedicimus tibi.

℟. Quia per sanctam Crucem tuam redemisti mundum.

℣. We adore Thee, O Christ, and we praise Thee.

℟. Because by Thy Holy Cross, Thou have redeemed the world.

A strong and therefore heavy Cross, for it is strong enough to bear Him on it when He arrives at Calvary, is placed upon His torn shoulders. He receives it gently and meekly, nay, with gladness of heart, for it is to be the salvation of mankind.

True; but recollect that heavy Cross is the weight of our sins. As it fell upon His neck and shoulders, it came down with a shock. Alas! What a sudden, heavy weight have I laid upon Thee, O Jesus. And though in the calm and clear foresight of Thy mind — for Thou seest all things — Thou wast fully prepared for it, yet Thy feeble frame tottered under it when it dropped down upon Thee. Ah! How great a misery is it that I have lifted up my hand against my God. How could I ever fancy He would forgive me, unless He had Himself told us that He underwent His bitter Passion in order that He might forgive us. I acknowledge, O Jesus, in the anguish and agony of my heart, that my sins it was that struck Thee on the face, that bruised Thy sacred arms, that tore Thy flesh with iron rods, that nailed Thee to the Cross, and let Thee slowly die upon it.

Pater, Ave, Gloria.

℣. Miserere nostri, Domine.

℟. Miserere nostri.

Fidelium animae, per misericordiam Dei, requiescant in pace. Amen.

Our Father, Hail Mary, Glory Be.

℣. Have mercy on us, O Lord.

℟. Have mercy on us.

May the souls of all the faithful departed, through the mercy of God, rest in peace. Amen.

Jesus Falls the First Time
beneath the Cross

℣. Adoramus te, Christe, et
benedicimus tibi.

℟. Quia per sanctam Crucem
tuam redemisti mundum.

℣. We adore Thee, O Christ, and we
praise Thee.

℟. Because by Thy Holy Cross,
Thou have redeemed the world.

Jesus, bowed down under the weight and the length of the unwieldy Cross that trailed after Him, slowly sets forth on His way amid the mockeries and insults of the crowd. His agony in the Garden itself was sufficient to exhaust Him; but it was only the first of a multitude of sufferings. He sets off with His whole heart, but His limbs fail Him, and He falls.

Yes, it is as I feared. Jesus, the strong and mighty Lord, has found for the moment our sins stronger than Himself. He falls — yet He bore the load for a while; He tottered, but He bore up and walked onward. What, then, made Him give way? I say, I repeat, it is an intimation and a memory to thee, O my soul, of thy falling back into mortal sin. I repented of the sins of my youth and went on well for a time; but at length a new temptation came when I was off my guard, and I suddenly fell away. Then all my good habits seemed to go at once; they were like a garment that is stripped off, so quickly and utterly did grace depart from me. And at that moment I looked at my Lord, and lo! He had fallen down, and I covered my face with my hands and remained in a state of great confusion.

Pater, Ave, Gloria.	Our Father, Hail Mary, Glory Be.
℣. Miserere nostri, Domine.	℣. Have mercy on us, O Lord.
℟. Miserere nostri.	℟. Have mercy on us.
Fidelium animae, per misericordiam Dei, requiescant in pace. Amen.	May the souls of all the faithful departed, through the mercy of God, rest in peace. Amen.

THE FOURTH STATION

Jesus Meets His Mother

℣. Adoramus te, Christe, et
benedicimus tibi.

℟. Quia per sanctam Crucem
tuam redemisti mundum.

℣. We adore Thee, O Christ, and we
praise Thee.

℟. Because by Thy Holy Cross,
Thou have redeemed the world.

Jesus rises, though wounded by His fall, journeys on, with His Cross still on His shoulders. He is bent down; but at one place, looking up, He sees His Mother. For an instant they just see each other, and He goes forward.

Mary would rather have had all His sufferings herself, could that have been, than not have known what they were by ceasing to be near Him. He, too, gained a refreshment, as from some soothing and grateful breath of air, to see her sad smile amid the sights and the noises that were about Him. She had known Him beautiful and glorious, with the freshness of divine innocence and peace upon His countenance; now she saw Him so changed and deformed that she could scarce have recognized Him save for the piercing, thrilling, peace-inspiring look He gave her. Still, He was now carrying the load of the world's sins, and, all-holy though He was, He carried the image of them on His very face. He looked like some outcast or outlaw who had frightful guilt upon Him. He had been made sin for us, who knew no sin; not a feature, not a limb, but spoke of guilt, of a curse, of punishment, of agony.

Oh, what a meeting of Son and Mother! Yet there was a mutual comfort, for there was a mutual sympathy. Jesus and Mary — do they forget that Passiontide through all eternity?

Pater, Ave, Gloria.	Our Father, Hail Mary, Glory Be.
℣. Miserere nostri, Domine.	℣. Have mercy on us, O Lord.
℟. Miserere nostri.	℟. Have mercy on us.
Fidelium animae, per misericordiam Dei, requiescant in pace. Amen.	May the souls of all the faithful departed, through the mercy of God, rest in peace. Amen.

Simon of Cyrene Helps Jesus to Carry the Cross

℣. Adoramus te, Christe, et benedicimus tibi.

℟. Quia per sanctam Crucem tuam redemisti mundum.

℣. We adore Thee, O Christ, and we praise Thee.

℟. Because by Thy Holy Cross, Thou have redeemed the world.

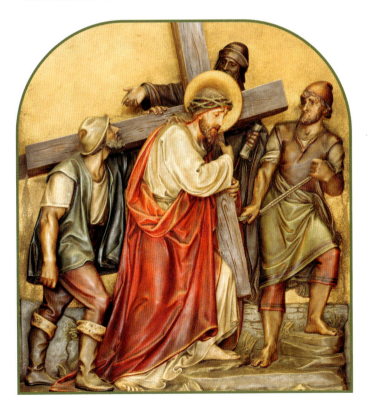

At length His strength fails utterly, and He is unable to proceed. The executioners stand perplexed. What are they to do? How is He to get to Calvary? Soon they see a stranger who seems strong and active — Simon of Cyrene. They seize on him and compel him to carry the Cross with Jesus. The sight of the Sufferer pierces the man's heart. Oh, what a privilege! O happy soul, elect of God! He takes the part assigned to him with joy.

This came of Mary's intercession. He prayed not for Himself, except that He might drink the full chalice of suffering and do His Father's will; but she showed herself a mother by following Him with her prayers, since she could help Him in no other way. She then sent this stranger to help Him. It was she who led the soldiers to see that they might be too fierce with Him. Sweet Mother, even do the like to us. Pray for us ever, Holy Mother of God, pray for us, whatever be our cross, as we pass along on our way. Pray for us, and we shall rise again, though we have fallen. Pray for us when sorrow, anxiety, or sickness comes upon us. Pray for us when we are prostrate under the power of temptation, and send some faithful servant of thine to succor us. And in the world to come, if found worthy to expiate our sins in the fiery prison, send some good angel to give us a season of refreshment. Pray for us, Holy Mother of God.

Pater, Ave, Gloria.	Our Father, Hail Mary, Glory Be.
℣. Miserere nostri, Domine.	℣. Have mercy on us, O Lord.
℟. Miserere nostri.	℟. Have mercy on us.
Fidelium animae, per misericordiam Dei, requiescant in pace. Amen.	May the souls of all the faithful departed, through the mercy of God, rest in peace. Amen.

THE SIXTH STATION

Jesus and Veronica

℣. Adoramus te, Christe, et benedicimus tibi.

℟. Quia per sanctam Crucem tuam redemisti mundum.

℣. We adore Thee, O Christ, and we praise Thee.

℟. Because by Thy Holy Cross, Thou have redeemed the world.

As Jesus toils along up the hill, covered with the sweat of death, a woman makes her way through the crowd and wipes His face with a napkin. In reward of her piety, the cloth retains the impression of the Sacred Countenance upon it.

The relief that a Mother's tenderness secured is not yet all she did. Her prayers sent Veronica as well as Simon — Simon to do a man's work, Veronica to do the part of a woman. The devout servant of Jesus did what she could. As Magdalene had poured the ointment at the Feast, so Veronica now offered Him this napkin in His Passion. "Ah," she said, "would I could do more! Why have I not the strength of Simon to take part in the burden of the Cross? But men only can serve the Great High Priest, now that He is celebrating the solemn act of sacrifice." O Jesus! Let us one and all minister to Thee according to our places and powers. And as Thou didst accept from Thy followers refreshment in Thy hour of trial, so give to us the support of Thy grace when we are hard pressed by our Foe. I feel I cannot bear up against temptations, weariness, despondency, and sin. I say to myself, what is the good of being religious? I shall fall, O my dear Savior, I shall certainly fall, unless Thou dost renew for me my vigor like the eagle's and breathe life into me by the soothing application and the touch of the Holy Sacraments that Thou hast appointed.

Pater, Ave, Gloria.	Our Father, Hail Mary, Glory Be.
℣. Miserere nostri, Domine.	℣. Have mercy on us, O Lord.
℟. Miserere nostri.	℟. Have mercy on us.
Fidelium animae, per misericordiam Dei, requiescant in pace. Amen.	May the souls of all the faithful departed, through the mercy of God, rest in peace. Amen.

Jesus Falls a Second Time

℣. Adoramus te, Christe, et benedicimus tibi.

℟. Quia per sanctam Crucem tuam redemisti mundum.

℣. We adore Thee, O Christ, and we praise Thee.

℟. Because by Thy Holy Cross, Thou have redeemed the world.

The pain of His wounds and the loss of blood increasing at every step of His way, again His limbs fail Him, and He falls on the ground.

What has He done to deserve all this? This is the reward received by the long-expected Messiah from the Chosen People, the Children of Israel. I know what to answer. He falls because I have fallen. I have fallen again. I know well that without Thy grace, O Lord, I could not stand; and I fancied that I had kept closely to Thy Sacraments; yet in spite of my going to Mass and to my duties, I am out of grace again. Why is it but because I have lost my devotional spirit and have come to Thy holy ordinances in a cold, formal way, without inward affection. I became lukewarm, tepid. I thought the battle of life was over and became secure. I had no lively faith, no sight of spiritual things. I came to church from habit and because I thought others would observe it. I ought to be a new creature, I ought to live by faith, hope, and charity; but I thought more of this world than of the world to come — and at last I forgot that I was a servant of God, and I followed the broad way that leadeth to destruction, not the narrow way that leadeth to life. And thus I fell from Thee.

Pater, Ave, Gloria.

℣. Miserere nostri, Domine.

℟. Miserere nostri.

Fidelium animae, per misericordiam Dei, requiescant in pace. Amen.

Our Father, Hail Mary, Glory Be.

℣. Have mercy on us, O Lord.

℟. Have mercy on us.

May the souls of all the faithful departed, through the mercy of God, rest in peace. Amen.

Jesus Comforts the Women of Jerusalem

℣. Adoramus te, Christe, et benedicimus tibi.

℟. Quia per sanctam Crucem tuam redemisti mundum.

℣. We adore Thee, O Christ, and we praise Thee.

℟. Because by Thy Holy Cross, Thou have redeemed the world.

At the sight of the sufferings of Jesus, the Holy Women are so pierced with grief that they cry out and bewail Him, careless what happens to them by so doing. Jesus, turning to them, said, "Daughters of Jerusalem, weep not over Me, but weep for yourselves and for your children."

Ah! Can it be, O Lord, that I shall prove one of those sinful children for whom Thou biddest their mothers to weep? "Weep not for Me," He said, "for I am the Lamb of God, and am making atonement at My own will for the sins of the world. I am suffering now, but I shall triumph; and, when I triumph, those souls, for whom I am dying, will either be my dearest friends or my deadliest enemies." Is it possible? O my Lord, can I grasp the terrible thought that Thou really didst weep for me — weep for me, as Thou didst weep over Jerusalem? Is it possible that I am one of the reprobate? Possible that I shall lose by Thy Passion and death, not gain by it? Oh, withdraw not from me. I am in a very bad way. I have so much evil in me. I have so little of an earnest, brave spirit to set against that evil. O Lord, what will become of me? It is so difficult for me to drive away the Evil Spirit from my heart. Thou alone canst effectually cast him out.

Pater, Ave, Gloria.

℣. Miserere nostri, Domine.

℟. Miserere nostri.

Fidelium animae, per misericordiam Dei, requiescant in pace. Amen.

Our Father, Hail Mary, Glory Be.

℣. Have mercy on us, O Lord.

℟. Have mercy on us.

May the souls of all the faithful departed, through the mercy of God, rest in peace. Amen.

THE NINTH STATION

Again, a Third Time, Jesus Falls

℣. Adoramus te, Christe, et benedicimus tibi.

℟. Quia per sanctam Crucem tuam redemisti mundum.

℣. We adore Thee, O Christ, and we praise Thee.

℟. Because by Thy Holy Cross, Thou have redeemed the world.

Jesus had now reached almost to the top of Calvary; but before He had gained the very spot where He was to be crucified, again He fell, and He is again dragged up and goaded onward by the brutal soldiery.

We are told in Holy Scripture of three falls of Satan, the Evil Spirit. The first was in the beginning; the second, when the gospel and the Kingdom of Heaven were preached to the world; the third will be at the end of all things. The first is told us by St. John the Evangelist. He says, "There was a great battle in Heaven. Michael and his angels fought with the dragon, and the dragon fought, and his angels. And they prevailed not, neither was their place found any more in Heaven. And that great dragon was cast out, the old serpent, who is called the devil and Satan" (Rev. 12:7–9). The second fall, at the time of the gospel, is spoken of by our Lord when He says, "I saw Satan, like lightning, falling from Heaven" (Luke 10:18). And the third by the same St. John: "There came down fire from God out of Heaven,... and the devil ... was cast into the pool of fire and brimstone" (Rev. 20:9–10).

These three falls — the past, the present, and the future — the Evil Spirit had in mind when he moved Judas to betray our Lord. This was just his hour. Our Lord, when He was seized, said to His enemies, "This is your hour and the power of darkness" (Luke 22:53). Satan knew his time was short and thought he might use it to good effect. But little dreaming that he would be acting in behalf of the world's redemption, which our Lord's Passion and death were to work out, in revenge and, as he thought, in triumph, he smote Him once, he smote Him twice, he smote Him thrice, each successive time a heavier blow. The weight of the Cross, the barbarity of the soldiers and the crowd, were but his instruments. O Jesus, the only-begotten Son of God, the Word Incarnate, we praise, adore, and love Thee for Thy ineffable condescension, even to allow Thyself thus for a time to fall into the hands and under the power of the Enemy of

God and man, in order thereby to save us from being his servants and companions for eternity.

Or this

This is the worst fall of the three. His strength has for a while utterly failed Him, and it is some time before the barbarous soldiers can bring Him to. Ah! It was His anticipation of what was to happen to me. I get worse and worse. He sees the end from the beginning. He was thinking of me all the time He dragged Himself along up the Hill of Calvary. He saw that I should fall again in spite of all former warnings and former assistance. He saw that I should become secure and self-confident, and that my enemy would then assail me with some new temptation to which I never thought I should be exposed. I thought my weakness lay all on one particular side that I knew. I had not a dream that I was not strong on the other. And so Satan came down on my unguarded side and got the better of me from my self-trust and self-satisfaction. I was wanting in humility. I thought no harm would come on me; I thought I had outlived the danger of sinning; I thought it was an easy thing to get to Heaven, and I was not watchful. It was my pride, and so I fell a third time.

Pater, Ave, Gloria.	Our Father, Hail Mary, Glory Be.
℣. Miserere nostri, Domine.	℣. Have mercy on us, O Lord.
℟. Miserere nostri.	℟. Have mercy on us.
Fidelium animae, per misericordiam Dei, requiescant in pace. Amen.	May the souls of all the faithful departed, through the mercy of God, rest in peace. Amen.

Jesus Is Stripped and Drenched with Gall

℣. Adoramus te, Christe, et benedicimus tibi.

℟. Quia per sanctam Crucem tuam redemisti mundum.

℣. We adore Thee, O Christ, and we praise Thee.

℟. Because by Thy Holy Cross, Thou have redeemed the world.

At length He has arrived at the place of sacrifice, and they begin to prepare Him for the Cross. His garments are torn from His bleeding body, and He, the Holy of Holiest, stands exposed to the gaze of the coarse and scoffing multitude.

O Thou who in Thy Passion wast stripped of all Thy clothes and held up to the curiosity and mockery of the rabble, strip me of myself here and now, that in the Last Day I come not to shame before men and angels. Thou didst endure the shame on Calvary that I might be spared the shame at the Judgment. Thou hadst nothing to be ashamed of personally, and the shame that Thou didst feel was because Thou hadst taken on Thee man's nature. When they took from Thee Thy garments, those innocent limbs of Thine were but objects of humble and loving adoration to the highest Seraphim. They stood around in speechless awe, wondering at Thy beauty, and they trembled at Thy infinite self-abasement. But I, O Lord, how shall I appear if Thou shalt hold me up hereafter to be gazed upon, stripped of that robe of grace that is Thine and seen in my own personal life and nature? Oh how hideous I am in myself, even in my best estate. Even when I am cleansed from my mortal sins, what disease and corruption is seen even in my venial sins. How shall I be fit for the society of angels, how for Thy presence, until Thou burnest this foul leprosy away in the fire of Purgatory?

Pater, Ave, Gloria.	Our Father, Hail Mary, Glory Be.
℣. Miserere nostri, Domine.	℣. Have mercy on us, O Lord.
℟. Miserere nostri.	℟. Have mercy on us.
Fidelium animae, per misericordiam Dei, requiescant in pace. Amen.	May the souls of all the faithful departed, through the mercy of God, rest in peace. Amen.

Jesus Is Nailed to the Cross

℣. Adoramus te, Christe, et benedicimus tibi.

℟. Quia per sanctam Crucem tuam redemisti mundum.

℣. We adore Thee, O Christ, and we praise Thee.

℟. Because by Thy Holy Cross, Thou have redeemed the world.

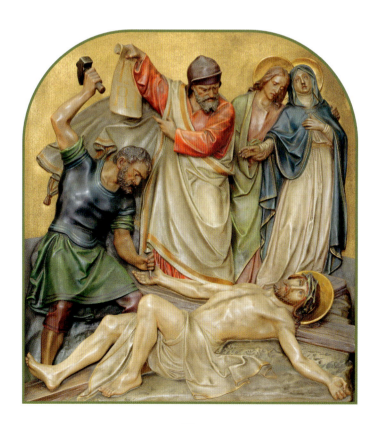

The Cross is laid on the ground, and Jesus stretched upon it; and then, swaying heavily to and fro, it is, after much exertion, jerked into the hole ready to receive it. Or, as others think, it is set upright, and Jesus is raised up and fastened to it. As the savage executioners drive in the huge nails, He offers Himself to the Eternal Father as a ransom for the world. The blows are struck — the blood gushes forth.

Yes, they set up the Cross on high, and they placed a ladder against it, and, having stripped Him of His garments, made Him mount. With His hands feebly grasping its sides and crosswoods, and His feet slowly, uncertainly, with much effort, with many slips, mounting up, the soldiers propped Him on each side, or He would have fallen. When He reached the projection where His sacred feet were to be, He turned round with sweet modesty and gentleness toward the fierce rabble, stretching out His arms as if He would embrace them. Then He lovingly placed the backs of His hands close against the transverse beam, waiting for the executioners to come with their sharp nails and heavy hammers to dig into the palms of His hands and to fasten them securely to the wood. There He hung, a perplexity to the multitude, a terror to evil spirits, the wonder, the awe, yet the joy, the adoration of the holy angels.

Pater, Ave, Gloria.	Our Father, Hail Mary, Glory Be.
℣. Miserere nostri, Domine.	℣. Have mercy on us, O Lord.
℟. Miserere nostri.	℟. Have mercy on us.
Fidelium animae, per misericordiam Dei, requiescant in pace. Amen.	May the souls of all the faithful departed, through the mercy of God, rest in peace. Amen.

THE TWELFTH STATION

Jesus Dies upon the Cross

℣. Adoramus te, Christe, et benedicimus tibi.

℟. Quia per sanctam Crucem tuam redemisti mundum.

℣. We adore Thee, O Christ, and we praise Thee.

℟. Because by Thy Holy Cross, Thou have redeemed the world.

Jesus hung for three hours. During this time, He prayed for His murderers, promised Paradise to the penitent robber, and committed His Blessed Mother to the guardianship of St. John. Then all was finished, and He bowed His head and gave up His Spirit.

The worst is over. The holiest is dead and departed. The most tender, the most affectionate, the holiest of the sons of men is gone. Jesus is dead, and with His death my sin shall die. I protest once for all, before men and angels, that sin shall no more have dominion over me. This Lent I make myself God's own forever. The salvation of my soul shall be my first concern. With the aid of His grace, I will create in me a deep hatred and sorrow for my past sins. I will try hard to detest sin as much as I have ever loved it. Into God's hands I put myself, not by halves but unreservedly. I promise Thee, O Lord, with the help of Thy grace, to keep out of the way of temptation, to avoid all occasions of sin, to turn at once from the voice of the Evil One, to be regular in my prayers, so to die to sin that Thou mayest not have died for me on the Cross in vain.

Pater, Ave, Gloria.	Our Father, Hail Mary, Glory Be.
℣. Miserere nostri, Domine.	℣. Have mercy on us, O Lord.
℟. Miserere nostri.	℟. Have mercy on us.
Fidelium animae, per misericordiam Dei, requiescant in pace. Amen.	May the souls of all the faithful departed, through the mercy of God, rest in peace. Amen.

Jesus Is Taken from the Cross and Laid in Mary's Bosom

℣. Adoramus te, Christe, et benedicimus tibi.

℟. Quia per sanctam Crucem tuam redemisti mundum.

℣. We adore Thee, O Christ, and we praise Thee.

℟. Because by Thy Holy Cross, Thou have redeemed the world.

The multitude have gone home. Calvary is left solitary and still, except that St. John and the holy women are there. Then come Joseph of Arimathea and Nicodemus, and they take down from the Cross the body of Jesus and place it in the arms of Mary.

O Mary, at last thou hast possession of thy Son. Now, when His enemies can do no more, they leave Him in contempt to thee. As His unexpected friends perform their difficult work, thou lookest on with unspeakable thoughts. Thy heart is pierced with the sword of which Simeon spoke. O Mother most sorrowful; yet in thy sorrow there is a still greater joy. The joy in prospect nerved thee to stand by Him as He hung upon the Cross; much more now, without swooning, without trembling, thou dost receive Him to thy arms and on thy lap. Now thou art supremely happy as having Him, though He comes to thee not as He went from thee. He went from thy home, O Mother of God, in the strength and beauty of His manhood, and He comes back to thee dislocated, torn to pieces, mangled, dead. Yet, O Blessed Mary, thou art happier in this hour of woe than on the day of the marriage feast, for then He was leaving thee, and now in the future, as a Risen Savior, He will be separated from thee no more.

Pater, Ave, Gloria.	Our Father, Hail Mary, Glory Be.
℣. Miserere nostri, Domine.	℣. Have mercy on us, O Lord.
℟. Miserere nostri.	℟. Have mercy on us.
Fidelium animae, per misericordiam Dei, requiescant in pace. Amen.	May the souls of all the faithful departed, through the mercy of God, rest in peace. Amen.

Jesus Is Laid in the Tomb

℣. Adoramus te, Christe, et benedicimus tibi.

℟. Quia per sanctam Crucem tuam redemisti mundum.

℣. We adore Thee, O Christ, and we praise Thee.

℟. Because by Thy Holy Cross, Thou have redeemed the world.

But for a short three days, for a day and a half, Mary then must give Him up. He is not yet risen. His friends and servants take Him from thee and place Him in an honorable tomb. They close it safely till the hour comes for His Resurrection.

Lie down and sleep in peace in the calm grave for a little while, dear Lord, and then wake up for an everlasting reign. We, like the faithful women, will watch around Thee, for all our treasure, all our life, is lodged with Thee. And when our turn comes to die, grant, sweet Lord, that we may sleep calmly too, the sleep of the just. Let us sleep peacefully for the brief interval between death and the general resurrection. Guard us from the enemy; save us from the pit. Let our friends remember us and pray for us, O dear Lord. Let Masses be said for us, so that the pains of Purgatory, so much deserved by us, and therefore so truly welcomed by us, may be over with little delay. Give us seasons of refreshment there; wrap us round with holy dreams and soothing contemplations while we gather strength to ascend the heavens. And then let our faithful guardian angels help us up the glorious ladder reaching from earth to Heaven that Jacob saw in vision. And when we reach the everlasting gates, let them open upon us with the music of angels; and let St. Peter receive us, and let our Lady, the glorious Queen of Saints, embrace us and bring us to Thee, and to Thy Eternal Father, and to Thy Coequal Spirit, Three Persons, One God, to reign with Them for ever and ever.

Pater, Ave, Gloria.	Our Father, Hail Mary, Glory Be.
℣. Miserere nostri, Domine.	℣. Have mercy on us, O Lord.
℟. Miserere nostri.	℟. Have mercy on us.
Fidelium animae, per misericordiam Dei, requiescant in pace. Amen.	May the souls of all the faithful departed, through the mercy of God, rest in peace. Amen.

Let Us Pray

GOD, WHO BY THE Precious Blood of Thy only-begotten Son didst sanctify the Standard of the Cross, grant, we beseech Thee, that we who rejoice in the glory of the same Holy Cross may at all times and places rejoice in Thy protection, through the same Christ, our Lord.

End with one Pater (Our Father), one Ave (Hail Mary), and one Gloria (Glory Be) for the intention of the Sovereign Pontiff.

About the Author

ST. JOHN HENRY NEWMAN (1801–1890) was born in London, became an Anglican clergyman, and led the Oxford Movement. When studying the history of the early Church Fathers, he began to consider Catholicism, withdrew from Oxford to pray for three years, and was received into the Roman Catholic Church by Blessed Fr. Dominic Barberi. During his elder years, he lived in the Birmingham Oratory, which he had founded, devoting his time to preaching, writing, and spiritual direction. In 1879, when Newman was seventy-eight, Pope Leo XIII made him a cardinal of the Holy Roman Church, as a tribute to his outstanding erudition and piety. Pope Francis canonized him in 2019.

Sophia Institute

SOPHIA INSTITUTE IS A nonprofit institution that seeks to nurture the spiritual, moral, and cultural life of souls and to spread the gospel of Christ in conformity with the authentic teachings of the Roman Catholic Church. Sophia Institute Press fulfills this mission by offering translations, reprints, and new publications that afford readers a rich source of the enduring wisdom of mankind.

Sophia Institute also operates the popular online resource CatholicExchange.com. *Catholic Exchange* provides world news from a Catholic perspective as well as daily devotionals and articles that will help readers to grow in holiness and live a life consistent with the teachings of the Church.

In 2013, Sophia Institute launched Sophia Institute for Teachers to renew and rebuild Catholic culture through service to Catholic education. With the goal of nurturing the spiritual, moral, and cultural life of souls, and an abiding respect for the role and work of teachers, we strive to provide materials and programs that are at once enlightening to the mind and ennobling to the heart; faithful and complete, as well as useful and practical.

Sophia Institute gratefully recognizes the Solidarity Association for preserving and encouraging the growth of our apostolate over the course of many years. Without their generous and timely support, this book would not be in your hands.

www.SophiaInstitute.com
www.CatholicExchange.com
www.SophiaTeachers.org

Sophia Institute Press is a registered trademark of Sophia Institute.
Sophia Institute is a tax-exempt institution as defined by the
Internal Revenue Code, Section 501(c)(3). Tax ID 22-2548708.